W9-BDW-493

INSIGHT FOR LIVING

── Broadcast Schedule ──

Letters to Churches:
Timeless Lessons for the Body of Christ

January 20–February 16, 1999

Wednesday	**January 20**	**Royal Mail in the Postman's Bag** *Revelation 1:1–20*
Thursday	**January 21**	**Royal Mail in the Postman's Bag**
Friday	**January 22**	**Everything but the One Thing** *Revelation 2:1–7*
Monday	**January 25**	**Everything but the One Thing**
Tuesday	**January 26**	**When Suffering Strikes** *Revelation 2:8–11*
Wednesday	**January 27**	**When Suffering Strikes**
Thursday	**January 28**	**Ministering Where Satan Dwells** *Revelation 2:12–17*
Friday	**January 29**	**Ministering Where Satan Dwells**
Monday	**February 1**	**Jezebel in the Church** *Revelation 2:18–29*
Tuesday	**February 2**	**Jezebel in the Church**
Wednesday	**February 3**	**A Church on Its Deathbed** *Revelation 3:1–6*
Thursday	**February 4**	**A Church on Its Deathbed**
Friday	**February 5**	**Open-Door Revival** *Revelation 3:7–13*
Monday	**February 8**	**Open-Door Revival**
Tuesday	**February 9**	**Our Number One Spiritual Battle** *Revelation 3:14–19*

Insight for Living • Post Office Box 69000, Anaheim, CA 92817-0900
Insight for Living Ministries • Post Office Box 2510, Vancouver, BC, Canada V6B 3W7
Insight for Living, Inc. • GPO Box 2823 EE, Melbourne, VIC 3001, Australia

Printed in the United States of America

Wednesday	**February 10**	**Our Number One Spiritual Battle**
Thursday	**February 11**	**Christ Is Knocking . . . Will You Answer?** *Revelation 3:30–22*
Friday	**February 12**	**Christ Is Knocking . . . Will You Answer?**
Monday	**February 15**	**Will You Lead or Lag?** *1 Corinthians 14:33; Exodus 18*
Tuesday	**February 16**	**Will You Lead or Lag?**

Letters to Churches

Timeless Lessons for the Body of Christ

BIBLE STUDY GUIDE

From the Bible-teaching ministry of

Charles R. Swindoll

INSIGHT FOR LIVING

Chuck graduated in 1963 from Dallas Theological Seminary, where he now serves as the school's fourth president, helping to prepare a new generation of men and women for the ministry. Chuck has served in pastorates in three states: Massachusetts, Texas, and California, including almost twenty-three years at the First Evangelical Free Church in Fullerton, California. His sermon messages have been aired over radio since 1979 as the *Insight for Living* broadcast. A best-selling author, Chuck has written numerous books and booklets on many subjects.

Based on the outlines and transcripts of Chuck's sermons, the study guide text is co-authored by Lee Hough, a graduate of the University of Texas at Arlington and Dallas Theological Seminary.

Editor in Chief:
Cynthia Swindoll

Director, Educational Ministries:
Gary Matlack

Coauthor of Text:
Lee Hough

Senior Editor and Assistant Writer:
Wendy Peterson

Copy Editors:
Marco Salazar
Glenda Schlahta

Text Designer:
Gary Lett

Graphic System Administrator:
Bob Haskins

Publishing System Specialist:
Alex Pasieka

Director, Communications Division:
John Norton

Production Manager:
Don Bernstein

Project Coordinator:
Shannon Scharkey

Printer:
Sinclair Printing Company

Unless otherwise identified, all Scripture references are from the New American Standard Bible, updated edition, copyright © The Lockman Foundation 1960, 1962, 1963, 1968, 1971, 1972, 1973, 1975, 1977, 1995. Used by permission. Scripture taken from the Holy Bible, New International Version © 1973, 1978, 1984 International Bible Society, used by permission of Zondervan Bible Publishers [NIV].

CONTENTS

1   Royal Mail in the Postman's Bag   1
    Revelation 1:1–20

2   Everything but the One Thing   12
    Revelation 2:1–7

3   When Suffering Strikes   20
    Revelation 2:8–11

4   Ministering Where Satan Dwells   28
    Revelation 2:12–17

5   Jezebel in the Church   37
    Revelation 2:18–29

6   A Church on Its Deathbed   45
    Revelation 3:1–6

7   Open-Door Revival   53
    Revelation 3:7–13

8   Our Number One Spiritual Battle.   61
    Revelation 3:14–19

9   Christ Is Knocking . . . Will You Answer?   70
    Revelation 3:20–22

10 Will You Lead or Lag?   77
    1 Corinthians 14:33; Exodus 18

    Books for Probing Further   86

    Notes   88

    Ordering Information   91

INTRODUCTION

Many Christians are surprised that some of the most practical truths in the New Testament are tucked away in the book of Revelation. This grand, final book of the Bible is more than a prophetic panorama of God's world program.

In the second and third chapters of Revelation, there appears a stack of letters—seven in all—addressed to first-century churches much like ones throughout our world. The relevance of these letters is nothing short of amazing. You will think the Spirit of God has been looking in on your church!

As we examine each letter and apply its contents to contemporary Christianity, let's be sensitive to the voice of God. Let's welcome His counsel, accept his evaluation, heed His warnings, and respond to His reproofs. In the final analysis, this is the only way we can lift the print off the pages of these inspired letters and incarnate the truth.

Chuck Swindoll

PUTTING TRUTH INTO ACTION

K nowledge apart from application falls short of God's desire for His children. He wants us to apply what we learn so that we will change and grow. This study guide was prepared with these goals in mind. As you go through the following pages, we hope your desire to discover biblical truth will grow as your understanding of God's Word increases and that you will be encouraged to apply what you've learned.

To assist you in your study, we've included a section called **Living Insights** at the end of each lesson. These exercises will challenge you to study further and to think of specific ways to put your discoveries into action.

There are many ways to use this guide—in personal devotions, group studies, discussions with friends and family, and Sunday school classes. And, of course, it's an ideal study aid when you're listening to its corresponding *Insight for Living* radio series.

To benefit most from this study guide, we would encourage you to consider it a spiritual journal. That's why we've included space in the **Living Insights** for recording your thoughts and discoveries. We hope you'll return to those sections often for review and encouragement as you continue to grow in your walk with Christ.

Lee Hough
Coauthor of Text

Letters to Churches

Timeless Lessons for the Body of Christ

The Seven Churches of Revelation 1–3

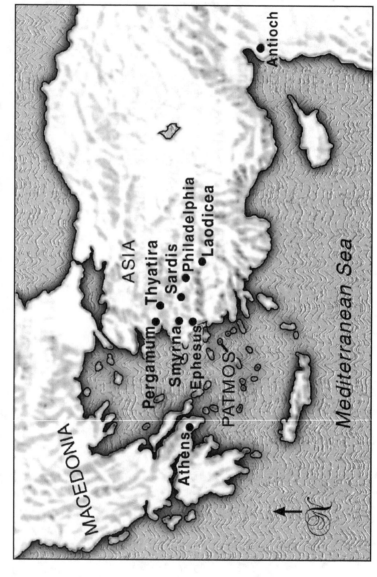

Chapter 1

ROYAL MAIL IN THE POSTMAN'S BAG
Revelation 1:1–20

Mail call!

Peterson . . . Matlack . . . Harris . . . Reader . . . reader? Oh, there you are. Special delivery for you: *Letters to Churches: Timeless Lessons for the Body of Christ.* So, you're going to study about the church? That's great, I remember the time when . . . huh? Who's it from? Well, let's have a look at the return address. Hmm, postage from Patmos and, ah yes, here it is—John, the Book of Revelation.

Whoa! You're not going to toss this, are you? Without even reading it? Oh, I see. If it were from Paul in Corinthians maybe, but John in Revelation? Nothing but "a riddle wrapped in a mystery inside an enigma,"[1] you think. So why bother, right?

If it's any reassurance, you're not the only one who feels this way. Many Christians view Revelation as a kind of biblical boogeyman. The name conjures up strange, incomprehensible images that scare away some of the most stouthearted of the faith. Sure, we all pay lip service to its being a part of God's inspired Word. *Just not a part of everyday life!* we really think. And certainly not the place we expect to find straightforward advice about the church.

Or so we think. But here's a new revelation: Jesus' royal mail to the church, especially in the first three chapters, is as piercingly relevant as any message you'll find in all the Scriptures. And the bonus is that the words are directly from the Lord's mouth.

---

1. Winston Churchill, as quoted in *Bartlett's Familiar Quotations*, 15th ed., rev. and enl., ed. Emily Morison Beck (Boston, Mass.: Little, Brown and Co., 1980), p. 743.

Interested? Good. Then let's open this letter together and allow the Spirit to write His own personal message about the church on our hearts.

Some Basic Observations: Revelation

Even though the Scriptures are God's personal word to every Christian, as we tear open the envelope to Revelation 1, we'll actually be reading someone else's mail. Mail that's nineteen centuries old! To find out who it belonged to, who wrote it, and why, let's pay careful attention to the letter's introductory comments.

Title

"The Revelation of Jesus Christ . . ." Scholars are not sure as to whether this five-word introduction means "The revelation *by* Jesus Christ" or "The revelation *concerning* Jesus Christ." The former implies that Jesus is going to reveal things to us; the latter means He is the One to be revealed. Without splitting hairs, the truth is that both are correct. Jesus is the *revealer*, as the rest of verse 1 shows: "The Revelation of Jesus Christ, which God gave Him to show to His bond-servants, the things which must soon take place." He is also the *revelation*, as indicated by the Greek word for revelation, *apokalupsis*, which means, "an unveiling" or "disclosure."[2]

To rephrase, then, the first five words mean: "The unveiling of Jesus Christ." And that's exactly what occurs over the entire scope of the book, as God pulls back the curtains on the future and allows a dramatic glimpse of His Son's second coming.

Recipient

Verse 1 also tells us to whom Christ gave His Revelation: "and He sent and communicated it by His angel to His bond-servant John." Which John, of course, is the question. Fortunately, church tradition has been consistent throughout the ages in affirming that this is none other than the disciple "whom Jesus loved," the apostle John (see John 13:23). His name appears on three other New Testament letters as well as a Gospel; but in this case, he's not technically

2. John F. Walvoord, "Revelation," in *The Bible Knowledge Commentary,* New Testament edition, ed. John F. Walvoord and Roy B. Zuck (Wheaton, Ill.: Scripture Press Publications, Victor Books, 1983), p. 928.

the author but more of a messenger. In summary, it is the

> revelation of Jesus Christ, which God gave Him to
> show to His bond-servants, the things which must
> soon take place; and He sent and communicated it
> by His angel to His bond-servant John, who testifies
> to the word of God and to the testimony of Jesus
> Christ, even to all that he saw. (Rev. 1:1–2)

Promise

> Blessed is he who reads and those who hear the
> words of the prophecy, and heed the things which
> are written in it; for the time is near. (v. 3)

The promise Christ holds out to those who read this book is almost identical to the one found in Luke 11:28, "Blessed are those who hear the word of God and observe it." The word *blessed* connotes happiness, deep satisfaction. From both of these passages it's clear Jesus means that only by taking the Scriptures to heart, meditating on them, and inviting the Spirit to reprove and correct our lives will we receive the blessing. Those who merely look at the words and walk away unchanged will receive no reward (see James 1:22–25).

Salutation

With this prologue of vital truths established, John now pens the opening lines of Christ's letter. But it is more than just a casual greeting. Encapsulated in these next few verses are the underlying themes and grandeur of all Revelation.

> John,
> To the seven churches in the province of Asia:
> > Grace and peace to you, from him who is, and
> who was, and who is to come, and from the seven
> spirits before his throne, and from Jesus Christ, who
> is the faithful witness, the firstborn from the dead,
> and the ruler of the kings of the earth.
> > To him who loves us and has freed us from our
> sins by his blood, and has made us to be a kingdom
> and priests to serve his God and Father—to him be
> glory and power for ever and ever! Amen.
> > Look, he is coming with the clouds,
> > and every eye will see him,

> even those who pierced him;
>   and all the peoples of the earth will
>   mourn because of him.
>   So shall it be! Amen.
> "I am the Alpha and the Omega," says the Lord
> God, "who is, and who was, and who is to come,
> the Almighty." (Rev. 1:4–8 NIV)

The recipients mentioned in this richly compacted salutation are seven churches located in the Roman province of Asia Minor (know today as Turkey). A familiar blessing is then followed by a grand procession of persons and truths. The church of the first century was accustomed to seeing Rome's power paraded in sweeping cavalcades of military might and glory. Now, John marshals forth a heavenly entourage of unsurpassable power and splendor.

First comes the unchangeable God; followed by the Spirit, who is represented in the seven Spirits present among the seven churches; and then Christ, the Savior, Ruler, Lamb of God. And trailing behind Him? You and me, "priests," saved sinners dedicated to serving and glorifying the Father. And it is to these priests of Asia, representatives of the church in all her strength and weakness throughout time, that John reveals the end of humankind's parade in the triumphant return of Christ.

Return Address

Next, John records several significant details about himself, such as where he was when he heard Jesus' words and how he came to be there.

> I, John, your brother and fellow partaker in the
> tribulation and kingdom and perseverance which are
> in Jesus,[3] was on the island called Patmos because
> of the word of God and the testimony of Jesus. (v. 9)

The apostle had been exiled to the isle of Patmos, a small, crescent-shaped chunk of rock (about sixteen square miles) located in the Aegean Sea, forty miles west-southwest of Miletus. The Emperor Domitian banished John there as a punishment for his "seditious" preaching in Ephesus (where he pastored) and as a quarantine to inhibit the further spread of the gospel.

---

3. Note that John here touches on three key themes—tribulation, the kingdom, and perseverance—which are woven throughout the message of Revelation.

Initial Communication: Jesus and John

Beginning in verse 10, John takes us back to the moment of his transcendent encounter with Jesus. He starts his amazing narrative with the brief statement, "I was in the Spirit." No one knows exactly what that means or how John came to be in that state. It's a mystery, frankly. Our best explanation is a description that says he was in an exalted state "in which the Seer is specially open to the Holy Spirit and ready to see visions"[4] (see also Rev. 4:2; 17:3; 21:10). Whatever it was, one thing is for sure. The apostle's mind and spirit were no longer bound to his body on Patmos.

When Did It Occur?

The vision took place, John says, "on the Lord's day" (1:10). Unfortunately, this expression is not used anywhere else in the entire New Testament, and John doesn't explain it either. Scholars speculate, however, that this phrase was a formal expression commemorating Christ's resurrection on the first day of the week. "As paganism had set aside a day on which to honor their emperor, so also Christians chose the first day of each week to honor Christ."[5]

What Was He Told to Do?

> And I heard behind me a loud voice like the sound of a trumpet, saying, "Write in a book what you see, and send it to the seven churches: to Ephesus and to Smyrna and to Pergamum and to Thyatira and to Sardis and to Philadelphia and to Laodicea." (vv. 10b–11)

John received two commands. First, to record all that he saw and heard, and, second, to send this revelation to seven churches located in Asia Minor (see map at front of guide). The seven churches were located in cities approximately thirty to fifty miles apart. Most likely, they are mentioned in the geographical order in which mail would have been delivered. So, despite Domitian's effort to silence John, God just made him postmaster general of Patmos to get His Word, come snow, rain, heat, or gloom of night, to Asia Minor and the world.

---

4. Leon Morris, *The Book of Revelation*, 2d ed., Tyndale New Testament Commentaries series (1987; reprint, Grand Rapids, Mich.: William B. Eerdmans Publishing Co., 1996), p. 52.

5. Robert H. Mounce, *The Book of Revelation*, The New International Commentary on the New Testament series (Grand Rapids, Mich.: William B. Eerdmans Publishing Co., 1977), p. 76.

Why Were These Seven Singled Out?

Why Smyrna instead of Philippi, or Sardis instead of Corinth or Rome? Surely there were bigger churches, more well-known and needy ones Christ could have chosen. But He didn't. Why? One popular answer contends that these seven churches symbolize seven consecutive periods in church history. The church at Ephesus, for example, represents the church of the apostolic era—doctrinally sound and bold, but lacking in love. Next, the church of Smyrna symbolizes the church's suffering in the postapostolic era of persecution. And on it goes down to the supposed lukewarm Laodicean church era of today.

The whole idea is fascinating, and there are some intriguing correlations, but . . . when you examine each era, you clearly find the merits and weaknesses of not one particular church but all seven! For example, during the time of the apostles, supposedly an era marked by doctrinal purity, the Galatian church compromised that purity in a way that exasperated the apostle Paul. And the Thessalonians endured intense struggles, something they weren't supposed to experience until the Smyrna era. Even today, theoretically an era of the lukewarm Laodicean church, we see many Ephesus-type assemblies boasting of a doctrinal purity that masks a lack of love toward the Savior and other people.

As you can see, what appears plausible at first becomes something forced and artificial in the end. But that's not the only reason we should avoid that interpretation. Spiritualizing the situations of the seven churches also minimizes the truth that these were real first-century churches with real strengths and weaknesses.

So why did Jesus choose these particular churches? Instead of dabbling in speculative answers, let's affirm three undebatable truths.

1. *Geographically*, they were readily accessible to one another and the world, especially with the city-port of Ephesus located right on the western coast of Asia Minor near Patmos.

2. *Historically*, these churches exemplified strengths Jesus wanted to commend and, except in Smyrna's and Philadelphia's cases, problems He wanted to correct.

3. *Spiritually*, churches of every age share the same strengths and weaknesses as those historical churches.

These messages, then, belong to the whole church throughout

6

time, which suffers, sins, and stands ready to serve the Lord, just like our first-century counterparts.

How Was This Revealed?

Now we come to the visually exciting part. After hearing the trumpetlike voice (v. 10), John turned to find out who was instructing him.

> Then I turned to see the voice that was speaking with me. And having turned I saw seven golden lampstands; and in the middle of the lampstands I saw one like a son of man, clothed in a robe reaching to the feet, and girded across His chest with a golden sash. His head and His hair were white like white wool, like snow; and His eyes were like a flame of fire. His feet were like burnished bronze, when it has been made to glow in a furnace, and His voice was like the sound of many waters. In His right hand He held seven stars, and out of His mouth came a sharp two-edged sword; and His face was like the sun shining in its strength.
>
> When I saw Him, I fell at His feet like a dead man. (vv. 12–17a)

John didn't speak, he didn't bow, he just hit the dirt. Wordless. His eyes glimpsed more than his heart could bear. Who was this celestial being whose presence prostrated the apostle in fear? This being reaches out to tell us and poor John, who is still lifeless at His feet.

> And He placed His right hand on me, saying, "Do not be afraid; I am the first and the last, and the living One; and I was dead, and behold, I am alive forevermore, and I have the keys of death and of Hades. Therefore write the things which you have seen, and the things which are, and the things which will take place after these things." (vv. 17b–19)

Our first glimpse of this divine person focuses on His majestic appearance (vv. 12–17a). Then we immediately see His magnificent mercy in offering John a reassuring touch (v. 17b). His description of Himself must have also brought comfort, as John quickly realized that this was none other than Jesus. Look carefully at the three statements He makes about Himself, so that there will be no doubt in your mind either. First, he mentions His eternal existence, "I am the first and the last"; then His death; and finally, His resurrection. Though God the Father and the Son both share the first characteristic (compare v. 8 with v. 17b), only the Son died on a cross for our sins and was resurrected three days later by the Father (see Acts 2:22–36). And that's when it hit John—Savior, Master, Jesus!

Like John, you may also be wondering what the lampstands and stars represent. Again, Jesus comes to our aid and explains.

> "As for the mystery of the seven stars which you saw
> in My right hand, and the seven golden lampstands:
> the seven stars are the angels of the seven churches,
> and the seven lampstands are the seven churches."
> (v. 20)

The meaning of the lampstands is clear, but theologians are still not quite sure who is meant by "the angels of the seven churches." Were they heavenly guardians? Perhaps, but then why would Jesus address angels if He wanted the churches to read the mail? Questions such as these, as well as the context of the passage, have led many commentators to identify the "angels" as the leaders of the individual churches: a pastor, a teaching elder, or a prophet. This is because the Greek word for *angel* (*angelos*, "messenger") is sometimes used in Scripture to refer to human messengers (see Matt. 11:7–10; Luke 9:52).

Personal Application

Moving from the first century to our own, three truths from John's Patmos experience still have tremendous practical significance for all of us who make up God's church today.

First, *Christ still stands in the center of His church.* Always remember what John saw. No matter how weak the church seems, how flawed or unfaithful, always remember that Christ stands in the center. "I will build My church; and the gates of Hades will not overpower it," Christ promised Peter (Matt. 16:18b). And His presence in the midst of those seven golden lampstands is a visual reminder, a welcome assurance, that we can depend on Him to keep that promise.

As Christians we believe that. But do we also believe that, as individual members of His church, we must also allow Him to be at the center of our lives? Where is he in your heart? Left of center? Extreme right? Center?

Second, *God still speaks through the authority of His Word.* What was it that John witnessed coming out of Christ's mouth? A sharp, two-edged sword. Listen to the writer of Hebrews as he beautifully elucidates the meaning behind the image.

> For the word of God is living and active and sharper than any two-edged sword, and piercing as far as the division of soul and spirit, of both joints and marrow, and able to judge the thoughts and intentions of the heart. (Heb. 4:12)

Has time dulled that sharp, piercing blade? Never. Will man-made religions blunt it? Not a chance. Can you depend on His Word? Absolutely. It is still timely, still relevant, still authoritative.

Third, *unfortunately, few still fall at His feet in honor and humility.* Hard to believe, isn't it? Of course, we've just come from reading about John's sublime vision of Jesus. Normally, our vision is clouded with TV shows and dirty dishes, soccer practices and grocery shopping. Not much sublime about our daily routines. So let's not be too hard on ourselves—at least not for the wrong thing. Sure, life is hardly beatific, but that doesn't mean we can't develop a sense of the sacred in the midst of it.

God speaks to us through all of life, not just when we're sitting in a pew or vacationing on an island. But in order to hear Him, we must learn to listen for Him in the ordinary . . . a note of encouragement from a friend—*Thank You, Jesus* . . . a reconciling hug from a child—*Praise You, Father.* These are but a couple of ways we can fall at the Savior's feet in praise and awe during our daily routine. You need not prostrate yourself on aisle six in the grocery store to give thanks for food, but you can whisper your gratitude as you fill your cart. As Victor Hugo once said,

> There are thoughts which are prayers. There are moments when, whatever the posture of the body, the soul is on its knees.[6]

---

6. Victor Hugo, *Les Misérables,* pt. 4, bk. 5, ch. 4 (1862), as quoted in *The Columbia Dictionary of Quotations,* comp. Robert Andrews (New York, N.Y.: Columbia University Press, 1993), p. 723.

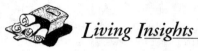 *Living Insights*

> Whom have I in heaven but You?
> And besides You, I desire nothing on earth.
> (Ps. 73:25)

Sometimes we get so caught up in examining John's heavenly vision that we tend to forget his nightmarish earthly existence. The aged disciple was isolated, exiled to Patmos. Imagine how lonely John must have felt, cut off from his church. How many times did he look out across the blue bars of his prison to the distant mountains of Asia Minor and wish he were home. Home! *Oh, to be involved in God's church again!* his heart ached. Then it would ache again, this time with the knee-buckling despair of knowing he was condemned to never experience that joy again. Domitian didn't send him to Patmos for a summer respite. He was in for life, and only death would send him home (or so Domitian intended).

Maybe you're experiencing a Patmos exile of your own. Unemployment. Divorce. A terminal illness. Rejection. Sometimes, even though we're not on an island, life can sure feel like it. People condemn us with their quick judgments, friends back away, loneliness steps in, and you feel cut off, perhaps even from God. John knows that feeling. And so does Jesus. He faced rejection too, remember? His own family, followers, and closest friends deserted Him.

In the depth of such pain, a desire crystallizes that surprises some. It is a desire greater than our need for a job or acceptance or relief. It's our desire for Jesus. We want Him, His love, His comfort.

Few people have expressed that raw passion more honestly than the struggling writer of Psalm 42. Let his words encompass and shape the yearning of your heart. Then, in your own words, ask the Lord to comfort, encourage, and embrace you as you study His Word in Revelation.

> As the deer pants for the water brooks,
> So my soul pants for You, O God.
> My soul thirsts for God, for the living God;
> When shall I come and appear before God?
> My tears have been my food day and night,
> While they say to me all day long, "Where is
> your God?"

These things I remember and I pour out my soul
within me.
For I used to go along with the throng and lead
them in procession to the house of God,
With the voice of joy and thanksgiving, a
multitude keeping festival.
Why are you in despair, O my soul?
And why have you become disturbed within me?
Hope in God, for I shall again praise Him
For the help of His presence. . . .
The Lord will command His lovingkindness in
the daytime;
And His song will be with me in the night,
A prayer to the God of my life.
I will say to God my rock, "Why have You
forgotten me?
Why do I go mourning because of the oppression
of the enemy?"
As a shattering of my bones, my adversaries
revile me,
While they say to me all day long, "Where is
your God?"
Why are you in despair, O my soul?
And why have you become disturbed within me?
Hope in God, for I shall yet praise Him,
The help of my countenance and my God.
(Psalm 42:1–5, 8–11)

_____

_____

_____

_____

_____

_____

_____

_____

Chapter 2

EVERYTHING BUT THE ONE THING

Revelation 2:1–7

Do you love me?"

In the wonderful musical *Fiddler on the Roof*, a Russian peasant named Tevye asks his wife this simple question.

Love him? Golde had never even met Tevye until the day of their arranged wedding. Now, after twenty-five years of marriage, he wants to talk of love? It sounds so, so . . . ridiculous, so foreign to her that she thinks he has indigestion and should lie down.

Tevye repeats the question, in earnest.

Golde wonders at his thinking, then explains how hard she has worked as his wife—cooking his meals, washing his clothes, having his children.

Still, it doesn't satisfy Tevye. So he asks again.

This time, Golde falls back on the obvious: she's his wife!

Even so, Tevye persists—does she love him?

After some reflection, she answers that she does indeed love him, realizing that her life hasn't been just meaningless busywork. She has worked so hard *because* of her love for Tevye.

It's possible, though, as Tevye realized and feared, for activity to *replace* love.

Another peasant, a first-century carpenter from Galilee, asks His Bride the same question Tevye asked his: "Do you love Me?" Does our full plate of activities show our fervent love for our Lord? Or are we so busy simply doing—Bible studies, evangelism, defending the faith, service, speaking—that our love for our Savior has grown cold?

That was the problem with the church in Ephesus. Their religious busyness (a status symbol in many churches today), rather than springing from a deep and joyful love for Christ, had effectively replaced their love for the Savior with an icy estrangement. So Jesus told the apostle John, "Write this down"—then He dictated a letter of generous praise but also of stinging rebuke.

Let's read the contents of His letter and, at the same time, allow the Spirit to read the contents of our lives to see if we are doing everything but the one thing—loving Him.

Background of Ephesus: The City and Church

To fully appreciate Christ's words to the church in Ephesus, we need to gain a clear picture of the geographical, cultural, and spiritual setting of this key Asian metropolis.

First, Ephesus was an important gulf city, located where the Cayster River met the Aegean Sea. As such, commerce flowed in and out of Ephesus, making it a crucial export center for much of Asia. In addition to the sea trade, the businesses of Ephesus profited from three main trade routes that converged there.

A visitor to this city would have been impressed not only with its hustle and bustle but also with its grandeur. Robert Mounce tells us that "the traveler from Rome landing at Ephesus would proceed up a magnificent avenue thirty-five feet wide and lined with columns which led from the harbor to the center of the city."[1] Though this splendid city was not Asia's capital (Pergamum was), it still held great political importance. The Roman governor tried important cases in Ephesus; and people flocked to its stadium, huge theater, and marketplace.

Ephesus, too, was a center for worshiping Rome's gods. Most famous of its temples was the temple of Artemis, also known as Diana (see how devoted to this goddess of love and fertility the Ephesians were in Acts 19:23–41). The epitome of Ephesian splendor, this temple was one of the seven wonders of the world.[2]

In this wealthy, politically influential, and pagan city, the apostle Paul first established a local congregation with the help of Priscilla, Aquila, and Apollos (see Acts 18:18–21, 24–26; 19:1–10, 17–20). Later, Paul left Timothy in his place to teach sound doctrine and guard against heresy (1 Tim. 1:3–4). Later still, tradition says that the apostle John was shipwrecked off Ephesus and stayed to serve there as a leader in the church until his exile on Patmos.

None of the other six cities mentioned in Revelation 2–3 held the prominence or history of this busy port. And bustling right along with it was the local church. It, too, held a long and distinguished history and was the most prominent church of the surrounding area.

---

1. Robert H. Mounce, *The Book of Revelation*, The New International Commentary on the New Testament series (Grand Rapids, Mich.: William B. Eerdmans Publishing Co., 1977), p. 85.

2. See Mounce, *The Book of Revelation*, pp. 85–86.

Introduction to the First Letter

> "To the angel of the church in Ephesus write:
> The One who holds the seven stars in His right
> hand, the One who walks among the seven golden
> lampstands, says this:
> 'I know your . . .'" (Rev. 2:1–2a)

Notice that Jesus "holds" the seven stars. It's the idea of holding the whole of something in one's hand, and it speaks of divine security, Christ's sovereign control. The leadership in each church is held firmly in His grip; a wonderful assurance and a sobering reminder.

Also, Jesus' walking "among the seven golden lampstands" represents His continual presence in His church. He visits the large and the small congregations, the liturgical and the casual. Everywhere His people gather, He is there. So the picture in verse 1 matches perfectly with Jesus' first words to the Ephesian church in verse 2: "I know your . . . ," implying, *I know you.*

Analysis of the Ephesian Christians

The One who continuously holds and probes His church now reports His findings in Ephesus.

Strengths: Areas of Commendation

> "'I know your deeds and your toil and persever-
> ance, and that you cannot tolerate evil men, and
> you put to the test those who call themselves apos-
> tles, and they are not, and you found them to be
> false; and you have perseverance and have endured
> for My name's sake, and have not grown weary.'"
> (vv. 2–3)

Jesus first commends their "deeds" and "toil." We would say the Ephesian church was *energetic and hard-working*. These believers lived in a city where cults flourished by decree and popularity. But instead of withdrawing, these committed Christians organized and ministered to the point of emotional and physical exhaustion. They helped birth their prayers into reality.

Jesus also applauds the Ephesians for their *hupomonē*, which is Greek for *perseverance* (vv. 2a, 3). William Barclay explains that this quality "is not the grim patience which resignedly accepts things, and which bows its head when troubles flow over it. *Hupomonē* is the courageous gallantry which accepts suffering and hardship and loss and turns them into grace and glory."[3] These Christians were marathoners, disciplined, determined, with a triumphant fortitude that undoubtedly harvested a rich spiritual bounty (compare Gal. 6:9).

Finally, Jesus compliments the Ephesians for their discernment and doctrinal purity (Rev. 2:2b), even praising them for their stand against one group in particular: the Nicolaitans (v. 6). Who were these people? D. M. Beck explains that they were possibly "a heretical sect, who retained pagan practices like idolatry and immorality contrary to the thought and the conduct required in Christian churches."[4]

Only a commitment to doctrinal purity could keep believers safe from those who would turn their freedom in Christ into bondage through sin or, at the other extreme, legalism. And the church at Ephesus successfully guarded her doctrinal purity. She would not flirt with frauds, she had no patience with apostates. Her jealousy for biblical truth shut the door on many a would-be suitor who might have compromised her principles.

Hard-working . . . persevering . . . discerning. Outstanding marks for any church, and the Ephesian believers beamed at such high praise.

"But . . ."

Weakness: Area of Condemnation

Hold on. Jesus isn't finished yet, and He has a bone to pick.

> "'But I have this against you, that you have left your first love.'" (v. 4)

Our greatest strengths can often become our greatest weaknesses. The Ephesians were the pit bulls of orthodoxy—guarding truth, chasing away false teachers. But in their zeal, they substituted knowledge for knowing, hating for loving. They knew how to defend the doctrines of the Word but forgot *Who* the doctrines pointed to. They forgot Jesus, their first love. All that was left was truth

---

3. William Barclay, *The Revelation of John*, 2d ed., The Daily Study Bible Series (Philadelphia, Pa.: Westminster Press, 1960), vol. 1, pp. 75–76.

4. D. M. Beck, as quoted by Mounce in *The Book of Revelation*, p. 89.

without grace. Law without love. A biting self-righteousness. So what might seem a silly question actually cuts to the heart of the problem.

"Do you love Me?"

"Yes, we rooted out all those who teach heresy."

"True. But do you love Me?"

"We fearlessly proclaim Your Word in spite of persecution."

"I know, I know. And that's good. But do you love *Me?*"

We already know the disappointing answer. And without that love for Jesus and for others, good deeds they were so proud of lost their real value (see 1 Cor. 13:1–3).

In 2 Corinthians 5:14, the apostle Paul wrote, "For the love of Christ controls us." *That's* to be our motivation in all that we do. *For the love of Christ,* persevere. *For the love of Christ,* do not tolerate those who corrupt the faith. The Ephesians, however, substituted "For the love of doctrinal purity" as their motto. And in the ebb and flow of their daily lives, that motivation eventually eroded their love till nothing was left but a cold orthodoxy.

Exhortation from the Living Lord

Could anything be done? The Ephesians' minds must have reeled with questions, remorse, maybe even fear. So Jesus offered them hope with these three exhortations.

First, "*Remember* from where you have fallen" (Rev. 2:5, emphasis added). The first step back for the prodigal son came when he remembered his home (see Luke 15:17). The first step back for the Ephesians would be to recall the sunny heights of enthusiasm and devotion to Christ that had marked the honeymoon of their love, to remember the intimacy and warmth, to reawaken the desire that had once been there.

Second, "*repent*" (Rev. 2:5, emphasis added). In other words, turn around! Don't keep going in the same direction. Confess that you've left your first love. And in your confessing, remember that repentance is not about blaming the circumstances or other people; it's about taking responsibility for your own wrongdoing and seeking forgiveness.

Third, "*do* the deeds you did at first" (v. 5, emphasis added). The Ephesians had become great at hating falsehood and lousy at loving Christ. They needed to recapture the joy of serving Christ out of a passionate love for Him.

In this letter, Jesus is generous in His praise, direct in His rebuke, helpful with a remedy, and completely no-nonsense about consequences if the Ephesians ignored His advice.

> "'Or else I am coming to you and will remove your lampstand out of its place—unless you repent.'" (v. 5b)

Any questions?

Application for the Believer Today

> "'He who has an ear, let him hear what the Spirit says to the churches. To him who overcomes, I will grant to eat of the tree of life which is in the Paradise of God.'" (v. 7)

Don't sit back now and make a detached analysis of Christ's commendations and condemnation to the Ephesians. Maybe He's speaking to you too. Are you listening—open? Or are you just hurrying through the motions of completing another Bible study so you won't be embarrassed if asked anything when the group meets?

Perhaps Jesus wants to commend you about your perseverance. Or maybe He has been trying to get your attention so that He can ask you one simple question:

"Do you love Me?"

 Living Insights

You knew we were going to ask this, didn't you? *Have you left your first love?* Does Christ's portrait of the Ephesian church look eerily familiar: diligent, courageous, zealous for the truth—yet loveless?

It's so easy to slip into sincere service that edges Christ out of our hearts, isn't it? To find ourselves embracing a Christian "lifestyle" but keeping Christ at an arm's distance. After living like this for a while, we become distracted, estranged, alienated from the One who is Love (1 John 4:8). And our works, which once reflected our love of Jesus, swing the spotlight to ourselves. We become more interested in people seeing our goodness, our being right. Pretty soon contempt replaces compassion, harshness supplants humility, self-centeredness suffuses service. How far we have fallen indeed.

Are we beyond hope? Of course not, or else Jesus wouldn't have confronted the Ephesian church and counseled them to repent. He wouldn't have promised a blessing for those who overcame their lovelessness if overcoming wasn't possible. So what do we need to do?

To begin with, we need to honestly evaluate our condition. Take this week, which is a gift from God to you, and reflect on what motivates your spiritual service. What drives your responses, your choices, your actions? What is under the surface of your life, deep in your heart? Come back to these pages during the next seven days to record what you find.

_____

_____

_____

_____

_____

_____

_____

_____

_____

_____

_____

_____

_____

_____

_____

_____

_____

_____

_____

_____

_____

_____

_____

No human motive will ever be completely pure. But did you find a leaning toward loving Christ at the heart of what you do? Or did these past seven days reveal a forgetfulness of Him?

_____

_____

_____

To resensitize yourself to His presence, you need to reorient your mind-set. You need to be aware of Christ, be attentive to Him. He needs to be your focus and priority. He once again needs to be included, as the apostle Paul says, in all that you do.

> Whatever you do in word or deed, do all in the name of the Lord Jesus, giving thanks through Him to God the Father. . . .
> . . . Whatever you do, do your work heartily, as for the Lord rather than for men, knowing that from the Lord you will receive the reward of the inheritance. It is the Lord Christ whom you serve. (Col. 3:17, 24–25)

In all things great, it is Christ whom you serve. In all things little, it is Christ whom you serve. In all things public, in all things private, in all things on the record, in all things off the record—it is Christ whom you serve. The applause or the obscurity doesn't matter. Because God—needing nothing—considers in our works only the love that accompanies them.

So meditate on Paul's words. And let Christ's Spirit make them your way of life, so that when He asks you, "Do you love Me?" you can answer with a heartfelt, "Yes!"

Chapter 3

WHEN SUFFERING STRIKES
Revelation 2:8–11

Love is a universal language. So is music. And so is suffering. They speak a dialect without words that is heard and understood by the soul. Only there, in the wordless lexicon of our hearts, are unspeakable ecstasy and unexplainable misery spoken and explained.

A friend once asked another, whose child had recently died, "How are you?" to which the father replied after a painful, groping pause, "I'll tell you . . . just as soon as I can find the words."

But there are none. Words cannot sound the depths of the suffering soul; the pain is too deep. Even in prayer, at times, the suffering becomes so intense that words fail and only a groan prevails. A syllable of suffering. The broken language of the soul.

The church at Smyrna understood such language. They were, by persecution and poverty, fluent in the dialects of hunger, loneliness, fear, and pain. So let's not open this next letter addressed to them with a half-hearted concern. For if we do, our hearts will be stone deaf to the One who intercedes with groanings too deep for words. We won't understand the language. We will miss the message.

But if we truly listen, strain to hear, then . . . then maybe we shall understand the hard consonants and guttural vowels of anguish shared between the sender and the receiver, whom suffering had tutored so well. And just maybe we will hear yet another universal language—encouragement—spoken to the hearts of the believers in Smyrna.

And, perhaps, to you.

Examination of a Personal Letter

Smyrna means "myrrh," or perfume, and indeed this redolent seaport located thirty-five miles north of Ephesus exuded a wealth and beauty that excited the senses. Known as "First of Asia,"[1] it boasted and backed up that claim with an excellent harbor, picturesque beauty, lavish temples, a famous stadium, and one of the

1. W. M. Ramsay, *The Letters to the Seven Churches*, updated edition, ed. Mark W. Wilson (Peabody, Mass.: Hendrickson Publishers, 1994), p. 185.

largest public theaters in Asia Minor. One of the few planned cities of antiquity, Smyrna's sweeping streets escorted you from its harbor through the narrow foothills up to Mount Pagos, which rose more than five hundred feet above the port. Necklaced around Pagos was a famous thoroughfare called the Street of Gold, whose beginning and end were marked by stately temples to Zeus and Cybele. Atop Mount Pagos gleamed the acropolis and numerous colonnaded buildings, which, by their magnificent appearance, earned the name "The Crown of Smyrna."

Heathen culture and pagan religion thrived with almost unparalleled splendor in Smyrna. Zeus, Hermes, Apollo, Dionysius, Mercury—the city hosted a banquet of gods from which to select for worship. Even Christ could have been added to the menu, but only after each individual had paid the price of publicly professing, "Caesar is Lord," and offering him sacrifice. The Christians in Smyrna refused to pay that blasphemous price and paid for it dearly, some with their lives.

From Christ to the Church

In the opening line of His letter to the Smyrnaean believers, Jesus immediately taps into the universal language of suffering and extends hope to a church near dead for thirst of encouragement.

> "And to the angel of the church in Smyrna write:
> The first and the last, who was dead, and has
> come to life, says this: . . ." (Rev. 2:8)

Why did Jesus choose this description of Himself? If you've ever suffered deeply, you probably already know. Who would best comfort a newly diagnosed cancer patient? A cancer survivor who's been there. Who would you want alongside you if you lost your spouse? Someone who's gone through a similar experience, someone who knows the hurt and how to help you through it. What did the hurting body of saints in Smyrna need? A sermon on perseverance? No, they needed someone who had been where they were, someone who understood the universal language of suffering and, in particular, the dark prose of persecution and poverty.

In those first few words, "who was dead," Jesus communicated volumes: *I've been where you are, I know what you're going through, I understand the pain and the fear*—words of reassurance and comfort (see also Heb. 4:14–16). Notice, too, the hope tucked away in the next phrase, "has come to life." For persecuted believers facing martyrdom, no one had to point out that word *life*. They caught it, clung to it, and it sent a glorious shiver of hope to the very depths of their souls.

Explanation of Their Condition

During periods of intense suffering, we often feel as though no one understands our pain. It is not enough, sometimes, for passersby to simply say, "I know how you feel." *Do you really?* we wonder, then doubt, and then fall deeper into a lonely despair. But to have someone actually name our pain with a clarity that removes all doubts about being understood—that frees us from the solitary confinement of our hurt and brings hope. Even if the suffering continues, we are at least given new strength to endure. Imagine, then, the comfort imparted in Jesus' next words:

> "'I know your tribulation and your poverty (but you are rich), and the blasphemy by those who say they are Jews and are not, but are a synagogue of Satan.'" (v. 9)

We must look at the Greek terms Jesus used to fully appreciate the depth of His insight into their condition.

He knew their tribulation, their *thlipsis*, a term used for affliction that originally "meant literal pressure, literal crushing beneath a weight. The pressure of events is on the church at Smyrna, and the force of circumstances is trying to crush the Christianity out of them."[2] Jesus saw that.

He also saw their extreme poverty, which he named *ptōcheia*. Two Greek words, *penia* and *ptōcheia*, designate poor people. One commentator elaborates, "The *penēs* has nothing superfluous, the *ptōchos* nothing at all."[3] What brought about such dire poverty? Many Christians in Smyrna were possibly slaves or belonged to the lower classes of society. Another, more sinister reason was that Christianity was illegal, which made it easy for Jews and pagans alike to plunder their businesses and ransack their homes and reputations with impunity.

2. William Barclay, *The Revelation of John*, 2d ed., The Daily Study Bible Series (Philadelphia, Pa.: Westminster Press, 1960), vol. 1, p. 95.

3. Trench, as quoted by Leon Morris in *The Book of Revelation*, 2d ed., Tyndale New Testament Commentaries series (1987; reprint, Grand Rapids, Mich.: William B. Eerdmans Publishing Co., 1996), p. 63.

Christ then offers a glimpse of hope with the contrasting reminder of their true riches in heaven (see also 2 Cor. 8:9). Notice that He doesn't deny their physical poverty—a devastating mistake many well-intentioned encouragers make. Rather, He provides them with a perspective for perseverance.

Last, Jesus addresses the slander instigated by the Jewish community. Commentator Michael Wilcock writes of this,

> The persecution at Smyrna was made especially poignant by the fact that the great enemy was the local community of Jews. These were God's people racially, but not really (Rom. 2:28), and were in fact blaspheming God as they persecuted his church under the guise of doing him service (Jn. 16:2). Perhaps it was economic pressure from these Jews that brought the church to poverty, and slanderous accusation by them (for "Satan" means "slanderer") that led to imprisonment and death.[4]

Encouragement as They Suffer

In addition to His empathy and intimate understanding of their struggles, Jesus now imparts courage for the trials ahead.

> "*'Do not fear* what you are about to suffer. Behold, the devil is about to cast some of you into prison, so that you will be tested, and you will have tribulation for ten days.[5] Be faithful until death. . . .'" (Rev. 2:10a, emphasis added)

"Do not fear." It is the Gospels' refrain. But from someone who's never been through your particular struggle, those words can sound empty, even contemptible. When they come from a kindred sufferer like Jesus, though, who has already been through what you're experiencing and has overcome, the words offer a reassurance that can stiffen even the weakest spine. Alone, we are afraid. But trusting in a scarred yet victorious Guide, we receive courage to face even our worst nightmares.

Jesus also speaks of remaining faithful even to death. I'm sure He would prefer to say, "until happier days"; but He knows a test of

---

4. Michael Wilcock, *The Message of Revelation: I Saw Heaven Opened*, The Bible Speaks Today Series (Downers Grove, Ill.: InterVarsity Press, 1975), pp. 45–46.

5. The "ten days" are generally considered to symbolize a short period of time.

supreme loyalty awaits them, so He warns instead. And by warning He gives His followers an unexpected grace that allows them to prepare for the coming flames.

Promises for Them to Claim

"Be faithful until death, and I will give you the crown of life" (v. 10b; see also James 1:12). Jesus is saying, in essence, "Don't be afraid to let go of this life, for an eternal life in heaven awaits you." Or as the battered, persecuted (and ultimately martyred) apostle Paul wrote,

> For momentary, light affliction is producing for us an eternal weight of glory far beyond all comparison, while we look not at the things which are seen, but at the things which are not seen; for the things which are seen are temporal, but the things which are not seen are eternal. (2 Cor. 4:17–18; see also Luke 9:23–26)

Jesus also gives the believers at Smyrna a second, related promise:

> "'He who has an ear, let him hear what the Spirit says to the churches. He who overcomes will not be hurt by the second death.'" (Rev. 2:11)

Jesus charges all seven of His churches in Revelation 2–3 with the command to overcome (see 2:7, 11, 17, 26; 3:5, 12, 21). In relation to the Smyrnaean church, we could interpret "overcome" as not succumbing to the temptation to save our own lives by deserting Christ. An earthly death pales in significance to a possible spiritual death—God's final judgment, the lake of fire (see 20:11–15). Those who are faithful to Christ are saved from this second death (see John 3:16).

One who did overcome was Polycarp, the Bishop of Smyrna, who was martyred in A.D. 155. During the Roman games, the riotous crowd shouted, "Away with the atheists! Find Polycarp!" Under torture, a poor slave told where Polycarp was staying, and the Roman guard came to arrest him.

Polycarp offered a meal to his enemies and asked for one last hour for prayer. Afterward, the reluctant Roman captain asked him, "What harm is there in saying, 'Caesar is Lord' and offering a sacrifice to save your life?" But for Polycarp, there was only one Lord, Jesus Christ.

24

When they got to the coliseum, the proconsul told him to choose Caesar and live, or choose Christ and die. Polycarp told him,

> "Eighty and six years have I served Him . . . and He has done me no wrong. How can I blaspheme my King who saved me?" The proconsul threatened him with burning, and Polycarp replied: "You threaten me with the fire that burns for a time, and is quickly quenched, for you do not know the fire which awaits the wicked in the judgment to come and in everlasting punishment. Why are you waiting? Come, do what you will."[6]

They did, and Polycarp was burned alive. But can you not read between the lines of his story the very words Christ wrote to the church at Smyrna years earlier? "Do not fear . . . be faithful . . . overcome . . . no second death." Polycarp lived that letter, personalized the principles so that even now, centuries later, his martyrdom reads like a testimony of encouragement.

Application for All Hurting Believers

"Where does it hurt?" Our parents used to ask us that when we were little, just as we ask our children, and just as our heavenly Father asks His children. Pause for a moment and allow the Spirit to apply these last two principles of encouragement as a salve to those areas of hurt in your life.

First, *remember that the Lord knows all about your circumstances.* Personalize verse 9 by inserting the particulars of your own suffering. For example, allow Jesus to say to you, "I know your worries about your daughter," or, "I know your pain of abandonment and betrayal." Speak the words out loud. Then, in prayerful silence, let Him impress the truth of those words upon your heart.

Second, *remember that if things get better, stay the same, or get worse, Jesus is always with us.* Circumstances cannot change Christ, because He "is the same yesterday and today and forever" (Heb. 13:8). Entrust yourself and your needs to the One who was persecuted, abandoned, crucified, and raised on your behalf. He "was dead, and has come to life." Welcome *Him*, not fear, into your heart.

---

6. Barclay, *The Revelation of John*, pp. 93–94.

The Tutsi and Hutu mothers in Rwanda whose children were slaughtered in a machete melee understand it as well as the mothers in Miami whose sons were killed in a drive-by shooting. Jews who survived the Holocaust understand it as well as Cambodians who survived the genocidal reign of the Khmer Rouge. The cancer patient in Russia understands it as well as the cancer patient in Romania or Rochester, New York. No matter what the country or culture, suffering teaches all its students the same basic alphabet.

What do we do with this second language that has been forced upon so many of us? Forget it as quickly as possible? Deny ever having learned it?

No. The universal language of suffering can be a *redemptive* language, something God uses to comfort others through us—if we do as the apostle Paul says in 2 Corinthians 1:3–4:

> Blessed be the God and Father of our Lord Jesus Christ, the Father of mercies and God of all comfort, who comforts us in all our affliction so that we will be able to comfort those who are in any affliction with the comfort with which we ourselves are comforted by God.

Comfort others as you have been comforted by God. Step into someone else's hurting world and speak the healing words God has taught you. Be His ambassador to the lonely, to the depressed, to the confused and hurting around you. Let Christ redeem your pain as He did Paul's by using it to comfort others.[7]

"Yes, well, I've never been through anything like Paul's afflictions, so how can I help others who have?" Fair question. Listen to the words of Walt Whitman: "I do not ask the wounded person how he feels, I myself become the wounded person."[8] If you can make those words your own, you will have taken a giant step toward learning the language of any individual's pain so that Christ may use you to bring His comfort.

---

7. To fully appreciate Paul's words in 2 Corinthians 1, read 2 Corinthians 11:23–28.

8. Walt Whitman, as quoted by Philip Yancey, in *Where Is God When It Hurts?* (Grand Rapids, Mich.: Zondervan Publishing House, 1977), p. 167.

In addition, what principles of encouragement did you pick up from this lesson?

_____

_____

_____

_____

_____

_____

_____

_____

_____

Before going on to the next lesson, take time to seek out the advice of others who have gone through difficult times. Ask questions like, What was most helpful? What was least helpful?

Finally, ask yourself this one question, Is there someone close to me with whom I can apply any of this?

Chapter 4

MINISTERING WHERE SATAN DWELLS

Revelation 2:12–17

Porno theaters. Plush offices paneled with cutthroat greed. Abortion clinics. Slums. Prisons of the deformed, the damned, the forgotten . . .

Satan has many strongholds. He has many places of retreat where the cacophony of human suffering soothes his twisted soul.

- Branch Davidian cults? A delightful bed-and-breakfast.

- Ethnic cleansing in Bosnia? An exhilarating sport!

- Hanging Christians in Saddam's Iraq? Real entertainment.

We cannot see Satan, yet his dwelling places carry the unmistakable marks of human suffering and moral perversion. Consider Nicolae Ceausescu's orphanages. Khmer Rouge killing fields. Russian gulags. Nazi concentration camps. The Spanish Inquisition. The chambers and instruments of torture throughout the Middle Ages. And—going all the way back to the first century—Rome's brutal slaughter of Christians.

One of Satan's favorite places in the Roman Empire was Pergamum. With its temples to *Dea Roma*, the goddess Rome, the spirit of Rome, it was *home* to Satan. A place of Roman imperial power backed by the Prince of the powers of darkness. Yet even there, in the Evil One's own backyard, Christians dared to play out their lives. Theirs was a courageous faith, a daring stronghold in the heart of enemy territory. Every day Satan pitched his forces against them in a frontal attack of persecution. And though he managed to kill and imprison a few individual Christians, he could not conquer the church.

At least not that way. In a clever change of tactics, he went gently knocking on the back door with a gift, a Trojan Horse called *compromise*.

That same knock can be heard in the life of every believer in every church in every city and every century. You hear it in that "little white lie," that rationalization for materialism, that indifference toward the poor, that excuse for not getting involved.

Do you hear knocking? Before you open the door, let's look through the window of Christ's letter to the church at Pergamum and see if it's a gift horse disguised as compromise.

Description of the Judge

The letter to the church at Pergamum, like all of Christ's letters to the churches, has its own unique introduction.

> "And to the angel of the church in Pergamum write:
> The One who has the sharp two-edged sword says this: . . ." (Rev. 2:12)

William Barclay gives us some historical insight into the significance of this image.

> Roman governors were divided into two classes—those who had the *ius gladii*, the right of the sword, and those who had not. Those who had the right of the sword had the power of life and death; on their word a man could be executed on the spot. Humanly speaking the proconsul, who had his headquarters at Pergamum, had the . . . right of the sword, and at any moment he might use it against any Christian; but the letter bids the Christian not to forget that the last word is still with the Risen Christ, who has the sharp two-edged sword. The power of Rome might be satanically powerful; the power of the Risen Lord is greater yet.[1]

Commentator John F. Walvoord brings out an additional shade of meaning:

> The sword is a symbolic representation of the Word of God's twofold ability to separate believers from the world and to condemn the world for its sin. It was the sword of salvation as well as the sword of death.[2]

1. William Barclay, *The Revelation of John*, rev. ed., The Daily Study Bible Series (Philadelphia, Pa.: Westminster Press, 1976), vol. 1, p. 90.

2. John F. Walvoord, "Revelation," in *The Bible Knowledge Commentary*, New Testament edition, ed. John F. Walvoord and Roy B. Zuck (Wheaton, Ill.: Scripture Press Publications, Victor Books, 1983), p. 936.

And it was this sword that Christ would wield to strike down compromise in the church at Pergamum.

Condition of the Church

As with each of His letters, Christ begins by affirming the strengths and struggles faced by that particular church.

> "'I know where you dwell, where Satan's throne is.'"
> (Rev. 2:13a)

Commendable Factors

"I know where you dwell." These believers put down roots in the kind of neighborhood most of us avoid at all costs. "Satan's throne," Jesus calls it, a place of satanic authority, a playground of demonic influence and spiritual oppression. Let's look at some of the reasons why.

In 133 B.C., Pergamum was named the capital of the Roman province of Asia and, as such, the official center of Caesar-worship. It was also one of the first cities in Asia to build a temple to Caesar Augustus. This set up the life-and-death tension between remaining true to Christ as Lord or capitulating to Roman pressure and confessing Caesar as Lord. For the loyal Christian, the threat of death loomed always.

"As Rome had become the center of Satan's activity in the West (cf. 13:2; 16:10), so Pergamum had become his 'throne' in the East."[3] Even the city's physical features boasted royal authority. Built on a tall, conelike hill, Pergamum towered over the valley below. From the top of it, you could see the Mediterranean Sea fifteen miles away. William Ramsay adds, "Beyond all other sites in Asia Minor it gives the traveler the impression of a royal city, the home of authority."[4]

In addition to its physical and imperial dominance, Pergamum had temples to Athena and Dionysus and a titan altar to Zeus. Satan loved it all, the religious splendor, the pagan practices. Added to this was its reputation as "the Lourdes of the Province of Asia."

---

3. Robert H. Mounce, *The Book of Revelation*, The New International Commentary on the New Testament series (Grand Rapids, Mich.: William B. Eerdmans Publishing Co., 1977), pp. 96–97.

4. W. M. Ramsay, *The Letters to the Seven Churches*, updated edition, ed. Mark W. Wilson (Peabody, Mass.: Hendrickson Publishers, 1994), p. 205.

People traveled from all over to be healed by the "the Pergamene god" *Asklepios Soter,* meaning "Asklepios the Savior," whose emblem was a serpent.[5]

Satan dwelt there, but so did Christ's Bride. Jesus emphasizes this fact with a Greek term for *dwell* that connotes permanence. Instead of running away to "greener subdivisions," safely ensconced from the evil of this world, these Christians deliberately put down roots in Pergamum. It seems they understood a basic principle so many today have forgotten: the Christian life is not escape—it's conquest. And Jesus commended them for it.

He also affirmed their fidelity in the face of martyrdom.

> "'And you hold fast My name, and did not deny My faith even in the days of Antipas, My witness, My faithful one, who was killed among you, where Satan dwells.'" (v. 13b)

Tradition has it that Antipas was roasted to death in a brazen bull. However he died, he died because he would not deny Jesus. And neither would the rest of the church. When pressed, they didn't flinch. When threatened, they didn't flee. When tested, they stayed true. How often today do Christians run from such places and pressures, always seeking lighter burdens rather than the strength to faithfully bear them.

Strong Criticism

The witness of the church stood as an unassailable fortress. Unfortunately, however, someone left a back door of compromise open.

> "'But I have a few things against you, because you have there some who hold the teaching of Balaam, who kept teaching Balak to put a stumbling block before the sons of Israel, to eat things sacrificed to idols and to commit acts of immorality. So you also have some who in the same way hold the teaching of the Nicolaitans.'" (vv. 14–15)

Commentator Robert Mounce explains the historical and moral ramifications of the phrase "teaching of Balaam."

It is clear from the context that this reference is not

5. Mounce, *The Book of Revelation,* pp. 95–96.

to a body of doctrine, but to Balaam's activity of advising the Midianite women how to beguile the Israelites into acting treacherously against the Lord. Numbers 25:1ff reports that the Israelites "began to play the harlot with the daughters of Moab," who in turn were successful in getting them to worship their gods and take part in their sacred meals. Although there is no mention of Balaam at this point, we learn in Numbers 31:16 of his role in Israel's apostasy (the Midianite women acted "by the counsel of Balaam"). . . . "Pagan food and pagan women were his powerful tools" [quoting commentator E. M. Blaiklock]. . . . Thus Balaam became a prototype of all corrupt teachers who betrayed believers into fatal compromise with worldly ideologies. . . .

. . . Nicolaitans are essentially the same group as the Balaamites. Both . . . accommodated [themselves] to the religious and social requirements of the pagan society in which they lived.[6]

Compromise, accommodation, and fitting in—the pressure of Balaam's teaching and the Nicolaitans' practices are just as real today as they were back then. Don't be so narrow-minded, "celebrate diversity," right? Many a church has lost its witness because it listened to the seductive voice of compromise. A voice that sounded to the believers at Pergamum, perhaps, much like this:

"Now, you are a man of broader understanding. You know very well that a few grains of incense have in themselves no importance whatever. Is not Christ within your heart? Has He not saved you by His grace? That is the important thing. Keep Christ within your heart by all means. But do not forget that you are a social being. You are not a hermit living out in the desert. This is Pergamos! And life in Pergamos makes certain demands on its citizens. If you do not wish, therefore, to find yourself ostracized from the social life of your city and to suffer

6. Mounce, *The Book of Revelation*, p. 98.

the disagreeable consequences which such a calamity would certainly have on your job, on your family, on your whole life, you cannot ignore the code of good manners of the citizens of Pergamos. Do come to the temple, be civilized. . . . It is only to a pleasant social function that I invite you."[7]

What could it hurt? According to Jesus, everything. Everybody. And He commands His Bride to end immediately her flirtatious affair with falsehood.

Correction of the Problem

"'Therefore repent; or else I am coming to you quickly, and I will make war against them with the sword of My mouth.'" (v. 16)

Christ's words must have startled those believers almost like a slap on the cheek, for in Greek, "Repent" rings out as a sharp command. "Wake up! Turn around! Do it now . . . immediately!"

Those who have been seduced by immorality and compromise will either repent and do it now or He will come with His "sword"—His Word, the truth—to judge and punish them for their sins.

Restoration of the Testimony

Jesus then quickly embraces His church with promised affirmations of His love.

"'He who has an ear, let him hear what the Spirit says to the churches. To him who overcomes, to him I will give some of the hidden manna, and I will give him a white stone, and a new name written on the stone which no one knows but he who receives it.'" (v. 17)

Three gifts are promised to those who *hear* and *overcome*. First, "hidden manna." One possible meaning pictured by this divine food is restored fellowship. If the church will stop eating the food of idol worship both in a metaphorical and real sense, Christ will feed them the true bread of heaven—Himself.

---

7. G. A. Hadjiantoniou, *The Postman of Patmos* (Grand Rapids, Mich.: Zondervan Publishing House, 1961), pp. 58–59.

Second, "I will give him a white stone." One plausible explanation of this image comes from an ancient practice of law. In Jesus' day, jurors would cast their vote to acquit someone by dropping a white stone into an urn. In the same way, Jesus promises a white stone denoting divine favor—acquittal, forgiveness—for those who overcome.[8]

And third, "a new name." Today names are chosen more for their aesthetic value than for their intrinsic meaning. In Jesus' day, however, a name was your identity; it was the verbal birthmark of your character. As a result of our repentance and perseverance, Jesus promises us a new name, signifying that He will reward us with a whole new identity.

Some Closing Thoughts on Compromise

Compromise never shows its face for what it is. It always projects itself as "a little white lie," "no big deal," "just having a little fun," "perfectly harmless." So it seemed to the church at Pergamum and, perhaps, to you. If you're tired of being conned by compromise, here are a few tips on how to stop this enemy from getting in the door.

First, always remember that *compromise never occurs quickly*. Just as water erodes, compromise erodes one innocuous drop at a time until there is a comfortable trickle, then an acceptable stream, and then an uncontrolled flood.

Second, *compromise always lowers the standard*. The flood never results in greater personal purity but always in deeper moral depravity. In other words, those we compromise with don't come up to the standards we hold, but we come down to the standards they're comfortable with.

Third, *compromise is seldom offensive*. Our tendency is always to judge sin by its outward appearance. Its real ugliness, however, is

---

8. Commentator Michael Wilcock offers another view of the white stone: "Since the context speaks of feasts of idol-meat and the feast of manna which God spread for Israel in the desert, perhaps the reference is to an ancient use of square stones as tickets of admission to some public entertainment. So the promise of eternal life which ends each of the first two Letters is repeated here in terms appropriate to the Christian who will not compromise with worldly pleasures and idol-meat banquets. Christ gives that man a personal invitation to the true pleasures of the banquet of heaven, which are, in fact, himself: for 'all the promises of God find their Yes in him,' and he is the true manna, the heavenly bread (2 Cor. 1:20; Jn. 6:31–35)." *The Message of Revelation: I Saw Heaven Opened*, The Bible Speaks Today Series (Downers Grove, Ill.: InterVarsity Press, 1975), pp. 48–49.

usually beneath the surface, in its intrinsic character. Andrew Bonar, Scottish preacher and author, once said, "It is not the importance of the thing, but the majesty of the Lawgiver, that is to be the standard of obedience."[9]

Finally, the wisdom of Bonar's words is affirmed in the truth that *compromise is often the first step toward total disobedience.* Compromise is never satisfied. It never stops after having gained an entrance. It just keeps coming, pushing the boundaries, wearing down resistance, until our lives resemble a once-plowed field now overgrown with weeds, reclaimed by the wild.

 Living Insights

Too often we rush into and out of studying biblical truth without allowing the Spirit the opportunity to speak to our own lives. Compromise loves that. It hides in the cracks of shallow thoughts and thrives in fruitless hurry. So let's slow down and prepare the soil of our hearts to receive the Spirit's truths by first reading and reflecting on two insightful quotes.

> Former presidential aide Jeb Stuart Magruder, commenting on the Watergate scandal, said, "We had conned ourselves into thinking we weren't doing anything really wrong, and by the time we were doing things that were illegal, we had lost control. We had gone from poor ethical behavior into illegal activities without even realizing it."[10]

Pause for a moment to consider any parallels to your own life.

> Every farmer knows the hunger of the wilderness, that hunger which no modern farm machinery, no improved agricultural methods, can ever quite destroy. No matter how well prepared the soil, how well kept the fences, how carefully painted the buildings, let the owner neglect for a while his prized

9. Andrew Bonar, as quoted by Jerry Bridges, in *The Pursuit of Holiness* (Colorado Springs, Colo.: NavPress, 1978), p. 23.

10. Jeb Stuart Magruder, as quoted by Jerry White, in *Honesty, Morality, and Conscience* (Colorado Springs, Colo.: NavPress, 1979), p. 83.

and valued acres and they will revert again to the wild and be swallowed up by the jungle or the wasteland. The bias of nature is toward the wilderness, never toward the fruitful field.[11]

As you reflect on these thoughts, write down whatever insights the Spirit may reveal. Are there some seen or unseen weeds of compromise popping up in your thought life, your business ethics, your marriage relationship, your finances, your personal purity, or your love for Christ?

_____

_____

_____

_____

How deep are the roots?

_____

_____

What will be necessary to pull them out by the roots?

_____

_____

_____

Who can help you? In what way?

_____

_____

_____

_____

11. A. W. Tozer, *The Root of the Righteous* (Camp Hill, Pa.: Christian Publications, 1955), p. 100.

Chapter 5

JEZEBEL IN THE CHURCH
Revelation 2:18–29

It stood like a lonely sentinel guarding an indefensible post. There were no hills to hide it, no great height to offer any fortified advantage. Yet it was charged with the heavy responsibility of being the gateway to Pergamum, the capital of the province. Armed with a garrison of Macedonian troops, the ancient city of Thyatira lay in the sweeping cradle of the Lycus valley, an easy, open target. At best, the defeat of this outpost might delay the enemy and give Pergamum more time to prepare to fight.

The attributes that made Thyatira a military disaster, however, also made it a commercial success. And, fortunately, at the time of Christ's letter to the church in this city, Thyatira's only invaders were friendly hordes of traders coming from Asia and the east. They advanced upon this frontier town along the same road that the imperial post traveled to Pergamum and Sardis, Philadelphia and Laodicea, Smyrna and Byzantium.

Thyatira was known for its numerous trade guilds—wool-workers, linen-workers, dyers (see Acts 16:14), leather-workers, potters, bakers, bronze-smiths—much more than for its military or spiritual significance. And yet, "the longest and most difficult of the seven letters is addressed to the least known, least important, and least remarkable of the cities."[1] Pliny, the historian, dismissed Thyatira as "unimportant."[2]

But not Jesus. He had a church there. And those believers were being attacked, not from the outside but from the inside, by one of their own—a woman who called herself a "prophetess." Jesus, however, called her a "Jezebel."

The Judge Described

Christ opens the letter to the church at Thyatira with still

---

1. Hemer, as quoted by Robert H. Mounce, in *The Book of Revelation*, The New International Commentary on the New Testament series (Grand Rapids, Mich.: William B. Eerdmans Publishing Co., 1977), p. 101.

2. William Barclay, *The Revelation of John*, 2d ed., The Daily Study Bible Series (Philadelphia, Pa.: Westminster Press, 1960), vol. 1, p. 125.

another unique vision of Himself, a vision that speaks directly to that church's problem and His power to overcome it.

> "And to the angel of the church in Thyatira write:
> The Son of God, who has eyes like a flame of fire, and His feet are like burnished bronze, says this: . . ." (Rev. 2:18)

This is the only letter, and the only place in all of Revelation, that mentions the title "the Son of God." By using it, Jesus immediately establishes His authority in the minds of the readers who were caught in a power struggle—one between Christ's way and a "new" way proposed by the prophetess.

Notice, too, the penetrating vision of His burning gaze. With searing discernment, Jesus sees past Jezebel's deceptive teaching. And with His bronze feet, strong and stern, He is ready to trample all the evil His eyes perceive.

The Church Revealed

Next we come to Christ's picture of the church.

In Its Strengths

> "'I know your deeds, and your love and faith and service and perseverance, and that your deeds of late are greater than at first.'" (v. 19)

Before focusing on the specifics of Christ's commendation, pause for a moment, with the help of Eugene Peterson, to reflect on the bigger picture—the "common outline" followed here and in all of the letters.

> Each [letter] is different in content but has a common outline that serves a common purpose: to provide spiritual direction to a people who are called to live by faith in Christ "in but not of the world." The spiritual direction begins with . . . first, a positive affirmation; second, a corrective discipline; and third, a motivating promise. In two of the churches (Sardis and Laodicea) the word of affirmation is omitted; in one (Smyrna) the course of discipline is absent. Otherwise, the three-part spiritual direction

is identical in each of the churches.[3]

We can learn much from Christ's approach with His churches. In contrast to His style, our way is to begin with a word of correction instead of affirmation. How often we barge into a situation or someone's life with scorching judgments, not knowing any details, not asking, just simply assuming. And that leads to nothing but strife. Whether with a son or daughter, a friend or someone at work, always remember the pattern of Christ's spiritual direction. Lead with the positive; affirm the good (see Prov. 15:23, 30).

For the church in Thyatira, the good is quite an impressive list of praiseworthy strengths: perseverance and ever-increasing deeds of service—all motivated by love and faith.

In Its Weakness

Despite this church's amazing spiritual growth, something is wrong; something deadly is growing inside this church body like a cancer.

> "'But I have this against you, that you tolerate the woman Jezebel, who calls herself a prophetess, and she teaches and leads My bond-servants astray so that they commit acts of immorality and eat things sacrificed to idols. I gave her time to repent, and she does not want to repent of her immorality.'" (Rev. 2:20–21)

With surgical precision, Christ's words cut right to the problem and lay it bare. First, He notes an attitude of tolerance that, like a moral malignancy, has been allowed to spread unchecked. The people have known it was there, have known it was wrong, and yet have refused to say anything about it. The wise words of Edmund Burke sum up the problem perfectly: "All that is necessary for the triumph of evil is that good men do nothing."[4]

Second, Jesus gives the cancer a name—Jezebel. For centuries, scholars have debated her true identity. Some conjecture that it was Lydia, who, before her conversion, was the seller of purple from Thyatira mentioned in Acts 16:13–15. That's just scandalous speculation. Others say Jesus refers to an actual woman named Jezebel. It sounds plausible, until you consider the history behind the name.

---

3. Eugene H. Peterson, *Reversed Thunder: The Revelation of John and the Praying Imagination* (1988; reprint, New York, N.Y.: HarperSanFrancisco, 1991), p. 50.

4. Edmund Burke, as quoted in *Knight's Master Book of New Illustrations*, comp. Walter B. Knight (Grand Rapids, Mich.: William B. Eerdmans Publishing Co., 1956), p. 430.

Jezebel was the wicked wife of Israel's most evil king, Ahab. She introduced Baal worship on a large scale, having 450 Baal prophets dine at her royal table regularly (1 Kings 18:19). She killed many of God's prophets and even tried to kill Elijah after he humiliated and destroyed her own prophets (v. 40; 19:1–2). She arranged the murder of an innocent man so her husband could gain his family property (chap. 21). And when she was finally killed in retribution for her sins, her dead body was eaten by the city dogs (2 Kings 9:30–37). No Jewish parents would shame their daughter and their family with such a name.

Other scholars have suggested that Jesus meant a "Jezebel condition." But the text says "woman." In light of that, perhaps the best interpretation is that this was an actual woman with a Jezebel-like character.

Third, Christ notes the particular characteristics of this cancer that made it so deadly: "They commit acts of immorality and eat things sacrificed to idols" (Rev. 2:20). Leon Morris give us deeper insight into the problem this New Testament Jezebel created.

> The powerful trade guilds in this city would have made it very difficult for any Christian to earn a living without belonging to a guild. But membership involved attendance at guild banquets, and this in turn meant eating meat which had first been sacrificed to an idol. What was the Christian to do? If he did not conform he was out of a job. *Jezebel* apparently reasoned that an idol was of no consequence . . . and advised Christians to eat such meals. That these meals all too readily degenerated into sexual looseness made matters worse.[5]

This Jezebel has taught expediency over principle, which has led others astray—and she has scorned Christ's gracious patience for repentance. Since the church has not confronted her, Jesus will.

> "'Behold, I will throw her on a bed of sickness, and those who commit adultery with her into great tribulation, unless they repent of her deeds. And I will kill her children with pestilence, and all the

5. Leon Morris, *The Book of Revelation*, 2d ed., Tyndale New Testament Commentaries series (1987; reprint, Grand Rapids, Mich.: William B. Eerdmans Publishing Co., 1996), pp. 70–71.

churches will know that I am He who searches the minds and hearts; and I will give to each one of you according to your deeds.'" (vv. 22–23)

Commentator Alan Johnson explores what these verses mean.

The "bed" or "couch" . . . can mean a bed used for resting, for guild-banqueting, or for sickness. . . . On a bed she sinned, on a bed she will suffer; and those who committed adultery with her will also suffer intensely. . . .

For those who follow Jezebel ("her children") and refuse to repent, a fatal judgment will be meted out by the Lord Jesus Christ. . . . Some understand "her children" to refer to her actual children, born of the sexual sins, rather than to her followers. . . . Whatever the exact nature of the judgment, it is announced beforehand by Christ so that when it occurs not just Thyatira but "all the churches will know that I am he who searches hearts and minds."[6]

The Saints Encouraged

Christ has given positive affirmation and corrective discipline; now He completes His letter to the church at Thyatira with motivating promises for the faithful.

"'But I say to you, the rest who are in Thyatira, who do not hold this teaching, who have not known the deep things of Satan,[7] as they call them—I place no other burden on you. Nevertheless what you

---

6. Alan F. Johnson, "Revelation," in *The Expositor's Bible Commentary*, gen. ed. Frank E. Gaebelein (Grand Rapids, Mich.: Zondervan Publishing House, Regency Reference Library, 1981), vol. 12, pp. 444–45.

7. "The deep things of Satan" could have referred to "the reasoning of some in the early church (the Nicolaitans) [which] might have gone something like this: The only effective way to confront Satan was to enter into his strongholds; the real nature of sin could only be learned by experience, and therefore only those who had really experienced sin could truly appreciate grace. So by experiencing the depths of paganism ('the deep secrets of Satan'), one would better be equipped to serve Christ, or be an example of freedom to his brothers (cf. 1 Cor 8:9–11). Thus the sin of Jezebel was deadly serious because of the depths of its deception. Only a few perceived where the teaching was leading." Johnson, "Revelation," pp. 445–46.

41

have, hold fast until I come. He who overcomes, and he who keeps My deeds until the end, to him I will give authority over the nations; and he shall rule them with a rod of iron, as the vessels of the potter are broken to pieces, as I also have received authority from My Father; and I will give him the morning star. He who has an ear, let him hear what the Spirit says to the churches.'" (vv. 24–29)

In verse 24, Jesus doesn't identify what is meant by "no other burden," but perhaps He's referring here to obedience. Surrounded by immorality, pressured by peers and the possible loss of their livelihood, Christ doesn't want to burden them with anything else besides an encouragement toward obedience.

For motivation, He promises two specific rewards: "authority over the nations" and "the morning star." The Lord focuses their eyes on the future, to His return, when the bright side of obedience will be fully realized as these faithful followers rule by His side in the coming kingdom. Even greater, however, will be the reward of the morning star, which Revelation 22:16 identifies as Jesus Himself. The One Whom they love, for Whom they suffer, to Whom they profess their love and loyalty, will finally be theirs in open, face-to-face fellowship and joy.

The Truth Applied

Unapplied truth is like medicine left in a bottle. It's there for the taking; you know that it will help; but instead, you simply ignore it, allowing the wound to worsen. The following four points are truths, medicine, gleaned from Christ's letter to the church at Thyatira. Take a moment to digest them and, with the space provided, to make some specific applications where needed in your own life.

First, *remember that big problems can occur in obscure places, so don't allow yourself to be caught unawares.*

_____

_____

_____

_____

Second, *remember that timely words can encourage discouraged people.*

_____

_____

_____

_____

Third, *remember that wrong teaching can come from gifted individuals. Don't be misled.*

_____

_____

_____

_____

And fourth, *remember that deceptive actions injure the innocent. If you find yourself caught up in deceptive teaching, don't be stubborn—repent!*

_____

_____

_____

_____

Living Insights

Did anything surprise you about the church at Thyatira? Something did me. Look back for a moment at the list of positive affirmations. Deeds, love, faith, service, perseverance, greater deeds now than at first. These were amazing people! Spiritual, committed, a city set on a hill.

And right in the middle was a black hole called Jezebel. Doesn't that strike you as just a little bit strange? I mean, if they were that mature, how could someone like her be tolerated, much less followed? Well, let's see if we can find the answer, not from the passage, but from our own lives.

Ask yourself, What have I tolerated? Fudging on your taxes?

Whitewashed, Christianized greed? Perhaps an undisciplined life-style; ethical violations; exposure to sexually explicit programs, films, or magazines? Too much flirting with a coworker?

You see, if we each look closely enough and are honest enough, the Spirit will gladly reveal to us where we have adopted an attitude of tolerance. Write down what the Spirit has revealed to you.

_____

_____

_____

_____

_____

Don't stop there. Now that you've identified some areas, ask yourself, Why do I tolerate these things? Is it for friendship? For financial gain? For prestige, maybe, or acceptance? Seek those answers, and you're grappling with some of the root issues that motivate your behavior.

_____

_____

_____

_____

_____

When you've identified some of them, ask yourself these two final questions: In what way does my tolerance reflect a lack of trust in Christ to meet my needs, and how can I turn this around?

_____

_____

_____

_____

_____

Chapter 6

A CHURCH ON ITS DEATHBED
Revelation 3:1–6

As unpleasant as it may seem, the opening of our next passage reads more like last rites than a letter. The body of believers living in Sardis was dead . . . almost. Only the faint pulse of a faithful remnant remained. For many, however, it was too late—their faith had flat-lined.

What begins as a deathbed scene, however, suddenly shifts to an emergency room drama. Rather than officiating over a funeral, Christ makes a last-ditch attempt to revive the hearts of the saints in Sardis.

Introduction to the Condition

"The town of Sardis lay about thirty miles south-east of Thyatira," writes commentator John Stott,

> and fifty miles due east of Smyrna. Situated at the foot of Mount Tmolus and in the fertile valley of the River Hermus, it was also the converging point of several inland roads, so that it had become a busy centre of trade and traffic. But its ancient history was more distinguished still. The capital of the old kingdom of Lydia, it was here that the fabulous King Croesus reigned amid his treasures until it fell to the swift attack of the Persian conqueror Cyrus.[1]

Persians, Greeks, Romans—Sardis had many conquerors, but none so devastating as the earthquake in A.D. 17 that leveled the city. To help rebuild, the Roman emperor Tiberius remitted all taxes for five years and donated 10 million sesterces.[2]

---

1. John Stott, *What Christ Thinks of the Church* (Wheaton, Ill.: Harold Shaw Publishers, 1990), p. 74.

2. According to Robert H. Mounce, 10 million sesterces would have been the equivalent of one million 1977 American dollars. *The Book of Revelation*, The New International Commentary on the New Testament series (Grand Rapids, Mich.: William B. Eerdmans Publishing Co., 1977), p. 109.

Sardis, then, flourished once more. Gold and silver coins changed hands in an open marketplace of decadent indulgence. The Greek historian Herodotus tells us that "the inhabitants of Sardis had over the course of many years acquired a reputation for lax moral standards and even open licentiousness."[3] Economically, they were rich; spiritually, they were bankrupt. Sadly, the church in Sardis, unlike Tiberius, had nothing to give to the needy culture around it.

So Jesus confronts them:

> "To the angel of the church in Sardis write:
> He who has the seven Spirits of God and the seven stars, says this: 'I know your deeds, that you have a name that you are alive, but you are dead.'"[4]
> (Rev. 3:1)

Jesus presents Himself to the church at Sardis, commentator Michael Wilcock explains, as having the "sevenfold Spirit," which represents "the eyes of God, from whom nothing is hidden (5:6) . . . also the life-giving power of God," and the seven stars, which symbolize "the angelic representatives of the churches." Jesus comes to these lifeless saints, then, as the One who "has in his hands both the needy church and the life-giving Spirit. He can bring the two together, not only to diagnose but also to revive the dead."[5]

What Jesus leaves out in His introductory words to the church at Sardis is as telling as what He includes. Notice that He doesn't mention

> anything like the persecutions at Smyrna and Pergamum or the heresies of the Nicolaitans. It may be that this church had not suffered disturbance from without and that its troubles stemmed from its comparatively sheltered existence. The temptation for

---

3. Stott, *What Christ Thinks of the Church*, p. 79.

4. Interestingly, one of Sardis' notable features "was the impressive necropolis, or cemetery, of 'a thousand hills' . . . so named because of the hundreds of burial mounds visible on the skyline some seven miles from Sardis." Alan F. Johnson, "Revelation," in *The Expositor's Bible Commentary*, gen. ed. Frank E. Gaebelein (Grand Rapids, Mich.: Zondervan Publishing House, Regency Reference Library, 1981), vol. 12, p. 447.

5. Michael Wilcock, *The Message of Revelation: I Saw Heaven Opened*, The Bible Speak Today Series (Downers Grove, Ill.: InterVarsity Press, 1975), p. 53.

the sheltered is always to take things easy, and they readily became slack.[6]

They had become so slack that it was hard to find any signs of life. So Jesus pronounces this body of believers as effectively dead. But take careful note of His words. Sardis has a "name," a respected reputation. "She is not what the world would call a dead church. . . . All regard her as a flourishing, active, successful church."[7] Like the Pharisees of Jesus' day, the church at Sardis had the appearance of great piety, but inside she was "full of dead men's bones and all uncleanness" (Matt. 23:27).

Did they offer prayers at Sardis? Yes. Did they sing songs of worship? Yes. Did they take offerings and perform good works? Yes and yes. Did they truly love Jesus? No. Sardis' reputation impressed only other people, not Jesus, who saw beneath the religiosity to the heart (see 1 Sam. 16:7). And it had stopped beating for Him.

Perhaps that explains why both Jews and Romans didn't bother this church. As Wilcock puts it,

> Content with mediocrity, lacking both the enthusiasm to entertain a heresy and the depth of conviction which provokes intolerance, it was too innocuous to be worth persecuting.[8]

Commands That Lead to Correction

If you've ever visited a hospital emergency room, you know that when the patient is wheeled in, commands fly in order to save that person's life. "Start an IV! Intubate! 100ccs of . . . now!" There's no time for, "Would you please," or, "When it's convenient." Doctors shout orders. Why? They're racing against death, and they may have only a few seconds lead.

For Sardis, there is no lead—spiritual death is imminent. What follows are five specific commands to resuscitate a failing church. Welcome to Christ's ER.

"'Wake up, and strengthen the things that remain,

---

6. Leon Morris, *The Book of Revelation*, 2d ed., Tyndale New Testament Commentaries series (1987; reprint, Grand Rapids, Mich.: William B. Eerdmans Publishing Co., 1996), pp. 74–75.

7. Wilcock, *The Message of Revelation*, p. 52.

8. Caird, as quoted by Morris in *The Book of Revelation*, p. 75.

which were about to die; for I have not found your deeds completed in the sight of My God. So remember what you have received and heard; and keep it, and repent.'" (Rev. 3:2–3a)

1. *Wake up!* This first command pictures an individual shaking someone who's going into shock, possibly a coma from which there is no return. "Don't pass out on me!" Stay awake—spiritually—and stay alive is the message. For the church at Sardis, Jesus means, "Be watchful of Satan's wiles and alert to God's presence in the present." He wants them to stop living on past experiences and to nurture a dynamic relationship that will act as a guard against the enemy's encroachment through false teaching or compromise (see 1 Cor. 16:13–14).

2. *Strengthen the remnant!* Next, Jesus immediately calls attention to the flicker of life that does remain. Keep it alive! Don't let it go out. Nourish and imitate the faithful few among you so that the entire church will eventually regenerate to become a healthy body again.

3. *Remember your purpose!* The Greek term for "remember what you have received and heard" (Rev. 3:3a) literally means, "Keep on remembering!" Never forget what you have received:

- The Good News—live it, share it.

- Faith—grow in it, defend it.

- Spiritual gifts—understand them, use them for service.

- Forgiveness—seek Christ's, and humbly extend it to others.

Jesus also urges them to never forget what they have heard: namely, His teachings as revealed and recorded by the writers of Scripture.

4. *Apply the truth!* Christ next orders a life-saving application of practical faith. Keep on applying the truth that you hear. Be doers of the word, not merely hearers (see James 1:22–25)! When you simply store up knowledge without applying it, your faith weakens and your resistance lowers to compromise.

5. *Change your direction!* The fifth and last command is simple: "Repent" (Rev. 3:3a). No more flirting with commitment; repent, change your direction, now! Doctor's orders.

And if the church at Sardis refuses? "I will come like a thief, and you will not know at what hour I will come to you" (Rev. 3:3b). Jesus leaves them with a warning whose point is all the more clear because of the history of Sardis. William Ramsay explains that the people had twice been conquered by stealth because they were overconfident of their security and unaware of their vulnerabilities.

The first time they were taken had been seven hundred years earlier. Back then, Sardis was a great city, so high up it was practically impregnable. However, during a siege by King Cyrus of Persia, Persian soldiers scrutinized the fortress walls and noticed an opening that had, "through want of proper care in surveying and repairing the fortifications . . . remained unobserved and unknown to the defenders."[9] So, at nightfall, this keen-eyed company climbed up and found the Sardian troops . . . gone. They were so confident in their position that they guarded the only expected entry but hadn't bothered to guard the other side of the fortress! Persian troops moved in swiftly, and Sardis was taken.

The second time this happened, 320 years later, Sardis fell to Antiochus the Great. "Once more the garrison in careless confidence were content to guard the one known approach, and left the rest of the circuit unguarded, under the belief that it could not be scaled."[10]

Promises for the Faithful

The emergency room commands have been given, and several life-saving truths have been injected. Now all Christ can do is wait and see how the patient will respond. But before He leaves, Jesus addresses the faithful remnant of the church.

> "'But you have a few people in Sardis who have not soiled their garments; and they will walk with Me in white, for they are worthy. He who overcomes will thus be clothed in white garments; and I will not erase his name from the book of life, and I will confess his name before My Father and before His angels. He who has an ear, let him hear what the Spirit says to the churches.'" (Rev. 3:4–6)

The few who have remained true to Christ receive three gracious promises.

---

9. W. F. Ramsay, *The Letters to the Seven Churches*, updated edition, ed. Mark W. Wilson (Peabody, Mass.: Hendrickson Publishers, 1994), p. 264.

10. Ramsay, *The Letters to the Seven Churches*, p. 265.

First, the promise of eternal righteousness: *You will walk with Me in white*. In other words, Jesus will clothe them with His purity. Soiled clothing, even in pagan religions, was believed "to dishonour the deity, so that those who wore soiled garments were debarred from worshipping."[11] But those who clung to Christ, who "washed their robes and made them white in the blood of the Lamb" (7:14), and who sought to remain unstained by the world, would wear Christ's worthiness. They would be clothed in Christ's purity and stand justified in the sight of God (compare Zech. 3).

Second, the promise of a place in heaven: *Your name will remain in the book of life*. That's security. Jesus will fulfill His promise to the remnant, His followers, that nothing can separate them from the Father (see John 10:27–29).

And last, Christ's own personal promise: *Your name will be announced before the Father*. "All these expressions help bring out the heavenly standing of those who belong to Christ. In highest heaven they have nothing to fear. When Jesus Christ vouches for anyone that person is accepted."[12]

Summary and Warning

When it comes to outward appearances, we are just as easily fooled by whitewashed religion as our first-century brothers and sisters. So how do we know what's real and what's a facade? Only Christ sees the heart . . . but perhaps we're not as blind as we may think. More likely, we are inattentive. Telltale signs are often there, only we're missing them. For example, consider these marks of a dying church.

- Worship of the past—when all the focus is on what God did years ago instead of declaring what God is doing today.

- Greater concern with form than with life—unwillingness to adapt, to find new ways of expressing biblical truth.

- Love of tradition over love for Christ—more concern for sacrifice according to man-made rules than a broken and contrite heart of compassion.

11. Moffatt, as cited by Morris in *The Book of Revelation*, p. 76.
12. Morris, *The Book of Revelation*, p. 76.

- Inflexibility and resistance to change—building altars to a certain way, time, or place, instead of to a living God whose Spirit defies all our attempts to fit Him into a certain pattern.

- Loss of evangelistic and missionary fervor—personal comfort cloaked as a matter of giftedness: "I'm just not as outgoing as she is."

If you're already experiencing some of the warning signs that indicate a dying faith, you don't have to stay that way. Want to be young again? Then recommit yourself to radical thinking—biblical thinking—and a willingness to change. No matter how "soiled" and unhealthy you may be, the Holy Spirit is always willing and able to bring life where before there was only death.

> Do you not know? Have you not heard?
> The Everlasting God, the Lord, the Creator of
>   the ends of the earth
> Does not become weary or tired.
> His understanding is inscrutable.
> He gives strength to the weary,
> And to him who lacks might He increases power.
> Though youths grow weary and tired,
> And vigorous young men stumble badly,
> Yet those who wait for the Lord
> Will gain new strength;
> They will mount up with wings like eagles,
> They will run and not get tired,
> They will walk and not become weary.
> (Isa. 40:28–31)

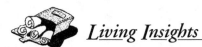 *Living Insights*

We all start with youthful enthusiasm when we first profess faith in Christ. But where are we now? Are we living out our faith based on the distant past? Are we simply going through the motions? Do we secretly harbor doubts and disaffection that only waits for the first crisis to defect?

Where are you? What signs of aging, if any, do you see? Are they signs of growing maturity and a greater spiritual life, or signs of deterioration and death? Pray before writing anything down. Pray for insight into your own condition; pause to allow the Spirit to bring things to mind in an attitude of prayer and submission. If what surfaces isn't healthy, pray, too, for the courage to admit yourself into His emergency room care as outlined in the lesson.

Condition: _____

_____

_____

_____

ER commands to follow: _____

_____

_____

_____

_____

_____

Chapter 7

OPEN-DOOR REVIVAL

Revelation 3:7–13

*K*atakekaumenē. No, that's not a Hawaiian king, it's a Greek word from the first century. It means "The Burned Land." Jesus addresses His sixth letter to the border town of Philadelphia, which sat on the edge of the *Katakekaumenē*, a fertile volcanic plain well suited to growing grapes and producing wine, both of which the city was well-known for.[1]

In addition to its agricultural success, Philadelphia prospered commercially. Situated at the eastern end of the same broad valley in which Sardis nestled, "this strategic location at the juncture of trade routes leading to Mysia, Lydia, and Phrygia . . . had helped it earn the title 'gateway to the East.'"[2]

Philadelphia was more, however, than just a gateway for economic prosperity. It was also an "open door" of opportunity—spiritually.

Description of the Savior

Jesus uses the words of the prophet Isaiah to introduce Himself to this church:

> "And to the angel of the church in Philadelphia write:
> He who is holy, who is true, who has the key of David, who opens and no one will shut, and who shuts and no one opens, says this: . . ." (Rev. 3:7)

As has been His pattern in each of His letters, Jesus establishes His own identity before encouraging the Philadelphian believers with three affirmations. First, He is "holy," meaning separate from sin, pure. Second, He is the "true" One. The Greek term for *true* connotes "real, genuine, the opposite of all that is false or deceitful."

---

1. See William Barclay, *The Revelation of John*, 2d ed., The Daily Study Bible Series (Philadelphia, Pa.: Westminster Press, 1960), vol. 1, p. 158.

2. Robert H. Mounce, *The Book of Revelation*, The New International Commentary on the New Testament series (Grand Rapids, Mich.: William B. Eerdmans Publishing Co., 1977), pp. 114–15.

And third, He is the sovereign One who holds "the key of David," who "opens and no one will shut, and who shuts and no one opens"—which is almost an exact quote from Isaiah 22:22.

In that passage, King Hezekiah's faithful servant, Eliakim, would replace the unfaithful Shebna and be given the high responsibility of carrying the keys to the royal palace. This position would put him second in authority to the king himself. No one could come in or go out except through him. He was in sovereign control of all entrances (see Isa. 22:20–24). In the same way, Jesus has complete control over the royal household of the heavenly kingdom. He is the sovereign gatekeeper and the door into God's sheepfold (John 10:9), His holy temple, heaven.

One who is pure, true, sovereign; "the Davidic Messiah with authority to control entrance to the kingdom."[3] That's who writes. Now let's find out the character of those He's writing to.

Condition of the Church

Unlike the dying church in Sardis, the church of Philadelphia is a sanctuary of spiritual vitality.

> "'I know your deeds. Behold, I have put before you an open door which no one can shut, because you have a little power, and have kept My word, and have not denied My name.'" (Rev. 3:8)

Let's look closely at the strengths reflected in Jesus' affirmations.

A *church of great opportunity*—"I have put before you an open door." Notice how the history of Philadelphia is woven into the meaning behind Christ's first comment.

> The intention of [Philadelphia's] founder was to make it a center of the Greco-Asiatic civilization and a means of spreading the Greek language and manners. . . . It was a missionary city from the beginning, founded to promote a certain unity of spirit, customs, and loyalty within the realm. . . . It was a successful teacher. Before A.D. 19 the Lydian tongue had ceased to be spoken in Lydia, and Greek

3. Robert Mounce, note on Revelation 3:7, in *The NIV Study Bible*, gen. ed. Kenneth L. Barker (Grand Rapids, Mich.: Zondervan Bible Publishers, 1985), p. 1930.

was the only language of the country.[4]

Now its missionary opportunity was far greater than spreading the Greek culture; it was strategically located to spread the life-changing gospel of Christ throughout Asia. All these believers had to do was step out in faith. Jesus was holding the door.

A *church of little power*—"you have a little power." This is not a word of criticism but simply a statement of fact, possibly referring to the size of the congregation or the social status of the church's members.[5] This characteristic makes the next trait of the Philadelphian church stand out all the more.

A *church of biblical fidelity*—"you . . . have kept My word." Small but faithful; that says it best. The church at Philadelphia succeeded where Sardis failed (see 3:2–3). No compromise, no departure, no apostasy. This small band of believers stayed true and genuine in their obedience to Christ.

A *church of good reputation*—"you . . . have not denied My name." Standing firm through the persecution of hostile Jews (see v. 9) resulted in a pure witness, unstained by defection to sin.

In a beautiful reflection, the Philadelphian believers mirrored the character of the One who wrote to them. When Jesus looked at them, He saw Himself. The church could receive no greater compliment, project no greater image.

Protection, Promises, and Blessings

Open doors, even if held by the Savior Himself, do not guarantee the absence of evil. We step through them to discover wonderful opportunities for service; but we also find new opportunities for selfishness and pride, defection or compromise. Evil opposition waits for spiritual progress at the threshold of every open door. It awaits the small band of Philadelphian believers like a lion crouched in hiding. Jesus can see the coming attack and offers four specific words of comfort.

First, *I, Jesus, will humble your enemies and open their eyes to the truth.*

"'Behold, I will cause those of the synagogue of Satan,

---

4. W. M. Ramsay, *The Letters to the Seven Churches*, updated edition, ed. Mark W. Wilson (Peabody, Mass.: Hendrickson Publishers, 1994), pp. 286–87.

5. See John Stott, *What Christ Thinks of the Church* (Wheaton, Ill.: Harold Shaw Publishers, 1990), p. 99.

who say that they are Jews and are not, but lie—I
will make them come and bow down at your feet,
and make them know that I have loved you.'" (v. 9)

As in Smyrna (2:9), one of the first adversaries to greet these
Christians at Christ's open door had been hostile Jews.

> Verse 9 takes us into the heart of a serious con-
> flict between church and synagogue in Philadelphia.
> The Jewish population was convinced that by na-
> tional identity and religious heritage it was the peo-
> ple of God. Not so, claimed the Christians. Had not
> Paul taught that "he is not a real Jew who is one
> outwardly. . . . He is a Jew who is one inwardly,
> and real circumcision is a matter of the heart" (Rom
> 2:28–29)? It was the church that could now be
> called "the Israel of God" (Gal 6:16), for the Jewish
> nation had forfeited that privilege by disbelief.[6]

What does Christ mean by saying He will make the unbelieving
Jews "bow down" (v. 9b)? For those of us unfamiliar with Jewish
thought and history, John Stott provides this helpful insight into
the meaning of the images Jesus uses. The Christless Jews

> are here portrayed as captives on the battlefield.
> They themselves would be familiar with this imag-
> ery. It had been prophesied of them years before that
> 'the sons of your oppressors will come bowing before
> you; all who despise you will bow down at your feet'
> (Isaiah 60:14). But now the tables are turned. In-
> stead of Gentiles kneeling at Jewish feet, Jews will
> bow down before Christians—not of course to wor-
> ship them, but humbly to recognize the community
> of Jesus as the new and the true Israel on whom God
> has set his love.[7]

Second, *I will keep you from maximum affliction.*

> "'Because you have kept the word of My persever-
> ance, I also will keep you from the hour of testing,

---

6. Mounce, *The Book of Revelation*, p. 118.

7. Stott, *What Christ Thinks of the Church*, p. 100.

that hour which is about to come upon the whole world, to test those who dwell on the earth. I am coming quickly; hold fast what you have, so that no one will take your crown.'" (vv. 10–11)

Commentators have long debated the precise meaning of this verse. Some assert that the "hour of testing" mentioned here refers to a coming persecution in the Philadelphians' day. It is unclear whether history has borne this out. Others contend that this is a prophetic reference to the end times' Tribulation. Still others believe that this is the day of God's judgment against those who have rejected Him, the Day of the Lord.

These differing ideas also color the interpretation of Christ's words, "I will keep you from the hour of testing." Some define "keep from," *tēreō ek* in Greek, as "keep through"—Christ is promising protection while either the Philadelphians go through a time of testing and/or we go through the Tribulation. Others believe that *from* here means "out from among," signifying a removal from trouble consonant with the idea of a pretribulation Rapture of the church. And still others maintain that believers will be protected spiritually from the day of God's wrath because of our salvation in Christ.

Whatever the case and however it is expressed, we can count on Christ's faithful, protective presence. In return, we are urged to remain steadfast in our faithfulness to Him and protect our precious heavenly reward.

Third, *I will make you strong and secure.*

"'He who overcomes, I will make him a pillar in the temple of My God, and he will not go out from it anymore.'" (v. 12a)

Once again, Christ's words speak to the history and hearts of the Philadelphians. That city

had suffered from earthquakes more than any other city of all Asia. In A.D. 17 a great earthquake had caused very serious damage; and the effects lasted for years after. . . . Two or three years later . . . shocks of earthquake were an everyday occurrence. The walls of the houses were constantly gaping in cracks. . . . Few people ventured to live in the city; most spent their lives outside, and devoted themselves to cultivating the fertile Philadelphian territory. . . .

Gradually, as time passed, people recovered confidence. . . . But when the seven letters were written the memory of that disastrous period was still fresh. People remembered, and perhaps still practiced, camping out in the open country. . . .

The concluding promise of the letter resumes this allusion: "Him who overcomes I will make a pillar in the temple of my God. Never again will he leave it." . . . The city which had suffered so much and so long from instability was to be rewarded with the divine firmness and steadfastness.[8]

Along with that coveted security was the promise of joy. For the temple was the place of God's presence (see Ps. 16:11).

Fourth, *I will give you a whole new identity.*

"'And I will write on him the name of My God, and the name of the city of My God, the new Jerusalem, which comes down out of heaven from My God, and My new name. He who has an ear, let him hear what the Spirit says to the churches.'" (Rev. 3:12b–13)

A new name meant a new identity; and this promise, too, had deep historical roots in the minds of its readers.

The people of Philadelphia would appreciate references to a new name more than most. While the name Philadelphia persisted, twice the city had received a new name: that of Neocaesarea, as a sign of gratitude for Tiberius's help in rebuilding after the earthquake, and later Flavia, after the family name of the emperor Vespasian.[9]

What kind of name (or names) would the overcomers of Philadelphia be getting? First, "the name of My God," which would signify that they belonged to God—He "had chosen to identify himself with them." Second, the name of "the New Jerusalem," which would assure them of their citizenship in the Messiah's eternal kingdom. And third, Christ's "new name," which could mean

8. Ramsay, *The Letters to the Seven Churches*, pp. 298–99.

9. Leon Morris, *The Book of Revelation*, 2d ed., Tyndale New Testament Commentaries series (1987; reprint, Grand Rapids, Mich.: William B. Eerdmans Publishing Co., 1996), p. 80.

"either the unknown name that he alone knows, signifying his absolute power over all other powers (19:12), or the new name of Christ given to the believer, i.e., his possession by Christ through redemption (Isa 62:2; 65:15)."[10]

A new name—not just a face-lift or a cosmetic alteration but a whole new identity. And Jesus promises that this one will last forever.

Conclusion and Application

Open doors. They come and we are grateful, excited, borne along in something we cannot explain yet know is from God. Then resistance hits. Sometimes from within; other times, without. Either way, it throws us. Suddenly we doubt ourselves, the open door, the future. Suddenly we find ourselves sinking in the very waves that once threatened Peter (see Matt. 14:22–31). The apostle James also wrote to remind us that "the one who doubts is like the surf of the sea, driven and tossed by the wind" (James 1:6b).

Having the faith to walk through those open doors and keep walking is not about plans, charts, graphs, marketing, or self-confidence. It's about faith in Him. It's about keeping His Word. It's about not denying Him in the face of persecution and suffering. It's about a little power. The power to take one small step at a time, with our eyes fully focused on Him.

Perhaps Jesus has an open door for you. Do you have the faith in Him to step through it?

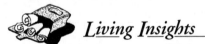 *Living Insights*

Jesus' words to the Philadelphians struck deep because they spoke to their past as well as their present. Perhaps His words touch something deep in you because they address something from your past. Think about it for a moment. Certainly Jesus wrote specifically to the Philadelphians, but then maybe this is His word to you, now, concerning your own history. Of the last four points from the lesson, which speaks most profoundly to you? How?

---

10. Alan F. Johnson, "Revelation," in *The Expositor's Bible Commentary*, gen. ed. Frank E. Gaebelein (Grand Rapids, Mich.: Zondervan Publishing House, Regency Reference Library, 1981), vol. 12, p. 455.

Chapter 8

OUR NUMBER ONE SPIRITUAL BATTLE
Revelation 3:14–19

Remember how you read the Scriptures as a young believer? Your relationship with Jesus was new, the love between you fresh. You wanted to know all about Him, to be with Him. And today, hopefully, that joy continues.

Sometimes, though, reading His Word is about as life-changing as reading the ingredient label on a cough syrup box.

Why does that happen? Listen to these wise words from Henri Nouwen.

> Reading the scriptures is not as easy as it seems since in our academic world we tend to make anything and everything we read subject to analysis and discussion. But the word of God should lead us first of all to contemplation and meditation. Instead of taking the words apart, we should bring them together in our innermost being; instead of wondering if we agree or disagree, we should wonder which words are directly spoken to us and connect directly with our most personal story. Instead of thinking about the words as potential subjects for an interesting dialogue or paper, we should be willing to let them penetrate into the most hidden corners of our heart, even to those places where no other word has yet found entrance. Then and only then can the word bear fruit as seed sown in rich soil.[1]

Who knows, maybe this was the problem with Laodicea. Like so many respectably religious Christians today, perhaps believers there fell into the habit of *using* the Scriptures only for proof texts and information rather than *receiving* them to get to know their Savior. The result? They were neither hot nor cold spiritually. Just

---

1. Henri J. M. Nouwen, *Reaching Out: The Three Movements of the Spiritual Life* (New York, N.Y.: Doubleday, Image Books, 1975), pp. 135–36.

respectably mediocre. Inoffensive. Bland. Lukewarm.

And that kind of tepid Christianity left Christ hot.

Some Background Information

Before we open Christ's scathing letter to the Laodicean church, let's briefly explore that ancient city and the surrounding area.

A wealthy city, Laodicea made the most of its enviable location. A number of major trade routes converged in its fertile valley, making it easy to export their renowned agricultural products. The glossy black sheep of the region, as one example, provided a high quality, soft wool used for clothing and carpets.

Also, Laodicea was a famed banking center. So wealthy were the inhabitants that when the A.D. 60 earthquake ravaged the area, the Laodiceans rebuilt their city on their own—with no financial aid from Rome.

One final significant note from history was the world-famous eye salve their medical school developed. Under the aegis of Asklepios, the god of healing, this temple-related school concocted an ointment from Phrygian powders designed to strengthen the eyes.[2]

For all its wealth and notoriety, however, Laodicea had one serious flaw, which, ironically, pictured the spiritual flaw of its wealthy church community. The only readily available water flowed "lime-laden . . . tepid and sickly, from nearby springs."[3] Laodicea had no "adequate [or] convenient source for water. . . . Thus water had to be brought in from springs near Denizli (six miles to the south) through a system of stone pipes."[4] The church was also "tepid and sickly" and desperately in need of the living water brought in through Jesus Christ (see John 4:7–14).

The Investigator: Jesus Christ, the Lord

Using three titles, Christ contrasts Himself with the lackadaisical church of Laodicea.

---

2. See John Stott, *What Christ Thinks of the Church* (Wheaton, Ill.: Harold Shaw Publishers, 1990), pp. 116, 118.

3. Michael Wilcock, *The Message of Revelation: I Saw Heaven Opened,* The Bible Speaks Today Series (Downers Grove, Ill.: InterVarsity Press, 1975), p. 57.

4. Robert H. Mounce, *The Book of Revelation,* The New International Commentary on the New Testament series (Grand Rapids, Mich.: William B. Eerdmans Publishing Co., 1977), p. 123.

"To the angel of the church in Laodicea write:
The Amen, the faithful and true Witness, the
Beginning of the creation of God, says this: . . ."
(Rev. 3:14)

First, Christ says He is "the Amen." William Barclay notes that

> in *Isaiah* 65:16 God is called . . . by the strange
> name the *God of Amen.* The word Amen is the word
> which is often put at the end of a solemn statement
> or affirmation in order to guarantee and to empha-
> size its truth. . . . This, then, would mean that
> Jesus Christ is the One whose words and promise
> are true beyond all doubt.[5]

Second, Jesus is "the faithful and true Witness." Some commentators have speculated that Jesus added this second title to help
clarify the meaning of the first for the non-Hebrew reader. Together
they mirror Christ's faithfulness to the apathetic Jews and Gentiles
of that church.

Third, Jesus is "the Beginning of the creation of God," a clear
reference to the words of Paul, "He is the image of the invisible
God, the firstborn of all creation" (Col. 1:15). Michael Wilcock
explains the significance of this last title.

> For the sake of this disastrous church, he presents
> himself in verse 14 as the beginning, or (less mis-
> leadingly) the origin, of God's creation, the one who
> is able to go right down into the chaotic abyss of
> Laodicea's failure and make her anew, as he once
> made the world.[6]

The Indictments and Evaluation

Christ now focuses His attention on describing the church at
Laodicea.

> "'I know your deeds, that you are neither cold
> nor hot; I wish that you were cold or hot. So because

---

5. William Barclay, *The Revelation of John*, 2d ed., The Daily Study Bible Series (Philadelphia,
Pa.: Westminster Press, 1960), vol. 1, pp. 176–77.

6. Wilcock, *The Message of Revelation*, p. 57.

you are lukewarm, and neither hot nor cold, I will spit you out of My mouth. Because you say, "I am rich, and have become wealthy, and have need of nothing," and you do not know that you are wretched and miserable and poor and blind and naked.'" (Rev. 3:15–17)

Notice that, for this church, Christ doesn't have a single word of commendation. Even Sardis had a small remnant worthy of praise. But not Laodicea. This is the only church for which Christ had nothing good to say. Let's take a closer look at what had gone wrong.

Condition of the Church

The Lord indicted the Laodicean believers on three counts.

First count: They were "neither cold nor hot" (v. 15a). This sums up the spiritual life of the church. For centuries, however, theologians have wrestled with the implication of that simple phrase. If we assume that "cold" and "hot" refer to the spiritual temperament of the church, then it leads us to the baffling conclusion that Jesus would prefer a "cold" church to one that is "lukewarm."

Some have argued convincingly that the key to understanding the contrast must be found in the ancient geography of that area. The nearby city of Hierapolis was famous for its hot medicinal springs; and Colossae, another neighbor, was known for its cold, pure water. Commentator Leon Morris draws the conclusion that "Hot water heals, cold water refreshes, but lukewarm water is useless for either purpose."[7] Could it be that Jesus was saying He found the church of Laodicea useless for either purpose as well?

Second count: They were "lukewarm" (v. 16). The Laodiceans had a mediocre, middle-of-the-road faith that affected or offended no one. They were like the tepid local water that unsuspecting visitors tasted and immediately spat out. Such a tepid religion caused a "moral nausea" in the Lord.[8]

Third count: They were unaware of their actual condition (v. 17). The spiritual acumen of the Laodicean church was reflected in the way they measured their Christianity by the balance of their

7. M. J. S. Rudwick and E. M. B. Green, as quoted by Leon Morris, in *The Book of Revelation*, 2d ed., Tyndale New Testament Commentaries series (1987; reprint, Grand Rapids, Mich.: William B. Eerdmans Publishing Co., 1996), p. 81.

8. Moffatt, as quoted by Mounce, in *The Book of Revelation*, p. 125.

bank account. "We have money; therefore, we have need of nothing." It's never a good idea, however, to estimate your spiritual condition by the size of your wallet. To emphasize the poverty of such thinking, Christ deliberately disparaged the very things that produced their wealth. He called them "beggars despite their banks, blind despite the Phrygian powders of their medical school, and naked despite their clothing factories."[9]

Reaction of the Lord

Tucked away at the end of verse 15, Christ provides a personal glimpse into His heart with the phrase, "I wish that you were cold or hot." The term used for *wish* expresses a fruitless desire, a vain wish. Perhaps it refers to the unsettling thought that He wishes they were either dead or alive rather than existing in a kind of comatose Christianity. Or maybe He's wishing their faith was cool and invigorating or hot and healing. Anything but blandly indifferent. That He will not tolerate.

His next thought is not a wish but a promise.

"'I will spit you out of My mouth.'" (v. 16b)

Nothing nauseates the Lord more than sacrifice without heart, words without meaning (see Prov. 21:3; 1 Sam. 15:22). The Laodiceans, in their blasé lukewarmness,

> were useless to Christ because they were compla-
> cent, self-satisfied, and indifferent to the real issues
> of faith in him and of discipleship. . . .
> Christ detests a Laodicean attitude of compromise,
> one that seeks easy accommodation and peace at any
> cost. With such a condition, he must deal harshly.
> To be a Christian means to be useful to Christ.[10]

The Laodiceans excelled at meeting a "minimum requirement" for being "acceptably" Christian—a little praying, a little Bible study and worship, a little evangelism, a little faith, a little love. The result? A spiritual farce. Something so revolting that Jesus could not stomach it.

9. Stott, *What Christ Thinks of the Church*, p. 118.

10. Alan F. Johnson, "Revelation," in *The Expositor's Bible Commentary*, gen. ed. Frank E. Gaebelein (Grand Rapids, Mich.: Zondervan Publishing House, Regency Reference Library, 1981), vol. 12, pp. 457–48.

Advice, Solution, and Application

To some, Christ's words may seem too severe, His analogy too graphic. No doubt the Laodiceans were stung by it, probably even angered. When we feel betrayed, hurt, or angry, we want to settle the score. Thank God, though, that Jesus' nature is to offer *grace*.

> "'I advise you to buy from Me gold refined by fire so that you may become rich, and white garments so that you may clothe yourself, and that the shame of your nakedness will not be revealed; and eye salve to anoint your eyes so that you may see. Those whom I love, I reprove and discipline; therefore be zealous and repent.'" (Rev. 3:18–19)

In place of wretched poverty, Jesus offers true gold, spiritual wealth that comes only when faith has been refined by fire and found trustworthy (compare 1 Pet. 1:7). In place of stark nakedness, Jesus offers white garments, a purity of character that only He can weave to cover a person's soul. In place of blindness, Jesus offers eye salve to restore their spiritual vision. He reassures them that He reproves and disciplines those He *loves* dearly. In return, He asks that they be "zealous and repent."

In his wonderful book *The Ragamuffin Gospel*, recovering alcoholic Brennan Manning writes,

> The philosophy of tough love is based on the conviction that no effective recovery can be initiated until a man admits that he is powerless over alcohol and that his life has become unmanageable. . . . In order to free the captive, one must name the captivity.[11]

There could be no effective recovery for the Laodiceans until they, too, admitted that, without Christ, they were powerless. The delusion of their lukewarm religion was like an alcoholic stupor. The situation called for tough love, for Someone who would fearlessly name the captivity in order to free the captive. We should all thank Him—on our knees—not only for loving the Laodiceans, but for loving us that way too. His love is our hope. Our only hope of freedom from sin.

11. Brennan Manning, *The Ragamuffin Gospel: Good News for the Bedraggled, Beat-Up, and Burnt Out* (Portland, Oreg.: Multnomah Press, 1990), p. 133.

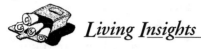 *Living Insights*

Pray for God's guidance before beginning.

With the help of John Stott, let's take Christ's letter to the Laodiceans out of the first century and apply it to today.

> Perhaps none of the seven letters is more appropriate to the church at the end of the twentieth century than this. It describes vividly the respectable, nominal, rather sentimental, skin-deep religiosity which is so widespread among us today. Our Christianity is flabby and anaemic. We appear to have taken a lukewarm bath of religion.[12]

Again we must ask the questions, Why is this happening? How does this happen? In his book *Shaped by the Word*, Robert Mulholland answers with an insightful look into today's culture.

> Ours is an objectivizing, informational, functional culture. We are largely governed by a materialistic/humanistic world view which perceives everything "out there" as something to be grasped, controlled, and manipulated for our own purposes. . . .
>
> The very thought of "being conformed"—which clearly implies that we are to be grasped, controlled, and shaped by someone other than ourselves—militates against our deeply ingrained sense of being. "Graspers" powerfully resist being grasped by God. Controllers are inherently incapable of yielding control to God. Manipulators strongly reject being shaped by God. . . . Information takers have extreme difficulty being receivers. Frenetically functional activists find it extremely difficult to "be still, and know" that God is God. . . .
>
> Genuine spiritual formation, being conformed, is the great reversal of the negative spiritual formation of our culture. It reverses our role from being the subject who controls the objects of the world,

---

12. Stott, *What Christ Thinks of the Church*, p. 114.

to being the object of the loving purposes of God who seeks to "control" us for our perfect wholeness.[13]

Does any of that speak to you? Can you see a glimpse of yourself in any of the five personality types Mulholland mentions? Which one(s), and how?

Grasper_____

_____

_____

Controller _____

_____

_____

Manipulator_____

_____

_____

Information taker _____

_____

_____

Frenetically functional activist_____

_____

_____

How about your approach to Scripture? Does it reflect one of the five personality types above? Before you leave this study, reread Henri Nouwen's words in the introduction. What specific applications will you draw for yourself in order to begin reading His Word for "formation" rather than merely "information"?

_____

_____

13. M. Robert Mulholland Jr., *Shaped by the Word: The Power of Scripture in Spiritual Formation* (Nashville, Tenn.: The Upper Room, 1985), pp. 28–29.

Chapter 9

CHRIST IS KNOCKING . . .
WILL YOU ANSWER?
Revelation 3:20–22

> "'Behold, I stand at the door and knock; if anyone hears My voice and opens the door, I will come in to him and will dine with him, and he with Me.'" (Rev. 3:20)

E veryone loves the intimate portrait Jesus paints of Himself in this familiar passage. We long to urge the world to open the door of their hearts, to welcome in the wonder of salvation and enjoy the pleasure of Jesus' company.

But oftentimes, we forget who Jesus was originally talking to and the context in which He spoke. And it is there that we find even more inviting truth.

This lovely picture of Christ standing at the door knocking is set in the black background of the lukewarm Laodicean church. This reality is an essential part of the picture Jesus wants framed in our hearts. Remember, Jesus had *nothing* good to say about this body of believers. He wanted to spew them out of His mouth, a violent image. And yet Christ then goes on to woo this spiritually nauseating church back to Himself with one of the most beautiful images of His grace in all the New Testament. For the Laodiceans! The wretched, miserable, poor, blind, naked Laodiceans. That's truly amazing grace.

Perhaps you hunger for that same grace. Certainly it would be safe and respectable to simply *study* the Laodiceans. But maybe what you're really needing, what you really want to know is, Can someone who's miserable spiritually and emotionally receive that same life-giving grace today, right now?

If this question uncovers a self-portrait you keep safely hidden, then come sit before His self-portrait so that He may transpose the timeless brushstrokes of His grace to the canvas of your heart. And when life seems overwhelming or meaningless, too painful to endure or depressingly lonely, let your heart trace the love Christ has put into every detail—for you.

A Mistaken Approach to Christ's Portrait

Intimate fellowship with Christ is certainly what we all need. Too often, however, we approach His Word with our analytical knife sharpened to dissect it into tiny pieces for scrutinizing and labeling. Though we may be able to accurately name all the parts, we miss the personal message of the whole as the Spirit means it for each of us.

In his book *Shaped by the Word*, Robert Mulholland does a little dissecting of his own—but this time with the intent of laying bare something in *us* rather than in the biblical text.

> We have a deeply ingrained way of reading in which *we* are the masters of the material we read. We come to a text with our own agenda firmly in place, perhaps not always consciously but usually subconsciously. If what we start to read does not fairly quickly begin to adapt itself to our agenda, we usually lay it aside and look for something that does. . . . *We* control *our* approach to the text; *we* control *our* interaction with the text; *we* control the impact of the text upon *our* lives.
>
> This mode of reading is detrimental to the role of scripture in spiritual formation. . . .
>
> In light of this situation, I would like to suggest to you . . . an alternate mode of approach to reading.
>
> First, I suggest that your top priority be to listen for God. Seek to allow your attention and focus to be on listening for what God is saying to you as you read. . . . Keep asking yourself, "What is God seeking to say to me in all of this?" By adopting this posture toward the text you will begin the process of reversing the learning mode that establishes *you* as the controlling power who seeks to master a body of information. Instead, you will begin to allow the text to become an instrument of God's control in your life.[1]

1. M. Robert Mulholland Jr., *Shaped by the Word: The Power of Scripture in Spiritual Formation* (Nashville, Tenn.: The Upper Room, 1985), pp. 21–22.

What "posture" are you bringing to the text of this lesson? As you enter Christ's sacred gallery in Revelation 3:20, are you willing to humbly ask, *What is God seeking to say to me?* The priceless portrait exhibited here is one that we may each hang above our broken lives to give hope—if—we have the right posture: a receptive heart.

Looking for the Artist within the Art

If you are ready, then look, listen, and receive Christ's masterpiece.

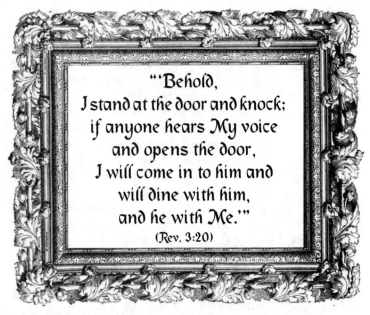

Look closely at the picture. What do you see? What do the details tell you about your Savior? About His amazing love for sinners? For you? Just before Jesus stood at the door, He said something extremely important to remember:

> "'Those whom *I love*, I reprove and discipline; therefore be zealous and repent.'" (v. 19, emphasis added)

Jesus isn't eager to condemn, to spit us out of His mouth. On the contrary, His love for us compels Him to care, to confront, to call us to come back to Him. For punishment? No, for clothing, healing, nourishment, companionship. For love. William Barclay helps us see into Jesus' heart as He stands before the door of our own hearts.

> Christ stands at the door of the human heart and knocks. The one unique new fact that Christianity brought into this world is the fact that God is the seeker of men. No other religion has the vision of a seeking God. In his book *Out of Nazareth* Donald Baillie cites . . . witnesses to the uniqueness of this amazing conception of a seeking God. Montefiore, the great Jewish scholar, said that the one thing which no Jewish prophet and no Jewish Rabbi ever conceived of is the "conception of God actually going out in quest of sinful men, who were not seeking Him, but who were turned away from Him." It would be great enough to think of a God who accepted men when they came back; it was beyond belief to think of a God who actually went out and searched. . . .
> Surely love can go no further than that.[2]

What do the eyes of your heart see now? What do you hear? Pause to write your reflections down in the Living Insights section at the end of this lesson.

Entering the Scene

To help those of you who might be struggling to receive Christ's portrait as anything but an abstract, first-century Picasso, let's take a moment to personalize the passage. Do you have a pen? Write your name in the following blank and then repeat the verse slowly a few times using the appropriate pronoun. You might even try giving emphasis to a different section of the verse each time you read it. Prayerfully seek Him. He promises to be found, just outside your door.

> "'Behold, I stand at the door and knock; if _____ hears My voice and opens the door, I will come in to him/her and will dine with him/her, and he/she with Me.'"

---

2. William Barclay, *The Revelation of John*, 2d ed., The Daily Study Bible Series (Philadelphia, Pa.: Westminster Press, 1960), vol. 1, pp. 185–86.

Again, pause to write down in the Living Insights section whatever thoughts the Spirit may be prompting in you about this verse. Take your time with this, it can make the difference between just gaining routine information and actually being formed in Christ.

Opening the Door

The beautiful picture of Revelation 3:20 comes with an amazing promise. *Open the door, and I will come in to dine with you. You open the door, and I will enter. We will eat together.* This "picture illustrates the shared joys of the Christian life, the reciprocal fellowship which believers have with their Savior."[3]

Christ enters, but not by force. He doesn't kick down the door of our lives; He gently knocks. He doesn't huff and puff with threats; He calls to *you*, the one He calls "beloved," no matter what you've done or how far from Him you've fallen. Surely love can go no further than that.

And if we hear His voice and open the door? Let us meet His love with our own. Love seeks to do "his will in his word and promptly to obey it," writes John Stott.

> It is not just attending religious services twice a Sunday or even every day, let alone on the major festivals. It is not just leading a decent life or believing certain articles of the creed. No, it is first to repent, turning decisively from everything we know to be wrong, and then to open the door to Jesus Christ, asking him to come in. It is getting our gold, our clothes and our eye salve from him. It is being personally and unconditionally committed to him. It is putting him first and seeking his pleasure in every department of life, public and private. Nothing less will do.[4]

Sitting next to Jesus

Jesus concludes this seventh letter as He did the six before—with a gracious promise to the overcomer.

---

3. John Stott, *What Christ Thinks of the Church* (Wheaton, Ill.: Harold Shaw Publishers, 1990), p. 122.

4. Stott, *What Christ Thinks of the Church*, pp. 122–23.

"'He who overcomes, I will grant to him to sit down with Me on My throne, as I also overcame and sat down with My Father on His throne. He who has an ear, let him hear what the Spirit says to the churches.'" (Rev. 3:21–22)

Not only did Jesus love the Laodicean church, not only did He knock at the door of their hearts and seek a welcome entrance, but He offered them the privilege of sitting with Him on His throne! All they had to do was repent and follow the way Jesus "overcame." Leon Morris emphasizes that the phrase "as I also overcame"

is important. Christ overcame by the way of the cross and this set the pattern for his followers.[5] (see John 16:33; 1 John 5:4)

The perils of the cross, the distinctiveness of belonging to Christ rather than blending in with the world, must be embraced before the Laodiceans—and we—can take a seat on Jesus' throne. As the apostle Paul wrote, we are "heirs of God and fellow heirs with Christ, if indeed we suffer with Him so that we may also be glorified with Him" (Rom. 8:17).

Do you see the nail prints on the hand that knocks on your heart's door? Letting Him in lets love in, with all its risks. But the end of His love is not the tenuous security of this world . . . but a place next to Jesus on the eternal throne of heaven.

So look, listen, and "hear what the Spirit says"—to *you*.

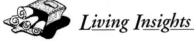 *Living Insights*

Use this space to record your thoughts as you work your way through the lesson.

_____

_____

_____

5. Leon Morris, *The Book of Revelation*, 2d ed., Tyndale New Testament Commentaries series (1987; reprint, Grand Rapids, Mich.: William B. Eerdmans Publishing Co., 1996), p. 84.

_____

_____

_____

_____

_____

_____

_____

_____

_____

_____

_____

_____

_____

_____

_____

_____

A final thought: Looking back at what you've written, what do you see? Are you still standing back from Christ's portrait, a mere spectator or critic? Or have you entered into it, stepped through the canvas and opened your heart to Him? The first approach only gathers information. The second transforms your life.

Chapter 10

WILL YOU LEAD OR LAG?

1 Corinthians 14:33; Exodus 18

Christ wrote seven letters to seven churches, each specifically addressed to "the angel of the church," meaning the leader or leadership shepherding that local body of believers.

He wrote to the Ephesian church's leader, who led a doctrinally pure assembly known for its uncompromising stand but which had lost their first love.

He wrote to the leader of the small church of Smyrna, which struggled in their suffering but had remained pure in their stand for Christ.

He wrote to the leader of the church in Pergamum, which remained faithful to Jesus' name yet tolerated a faction that taught doctrinal compromise.

He wrote to the leader of the church in Thyatira, which was known for their love, faith, service, and perseverance—and for their moral compromise.

He wrote to the leader of the church in Sardis: a big, impressive, well-known church—but on its deathbed.

He wrote to the angel of the church in Philadelphia: a vital church with a door of spiritual opportunity opened before her.

He wrote to the leader of the church in Laodicea, which was indistinguishable from the culture around it and whose attitude nauseated the Lord.

Before closing this study, it would be beneficial to look at yet one more letter, this one from the apostle Paul to the church in Corinth. In it, he lays down one of God's foundational "bricks" for building sound leadership for a strong church.

A Statement of What Pleases God

First Corinthians 14 is Paul's attempt to correct the disorder and confusion that was present in the first-century church at Corinth. Although we won't be studying that church's problems in

This chapter has been adapted from the study guide *Questions Christians Ask,* coauthored by David Lien, with Living Insights by Lee Hough, from the Bible-teaching ministry of Charles R. Swindoll (Fullerton, Calif.: Insight for Living, 1989), pp. 59–66.

this lesson, we can learn some important information about God from Paul's words in verse 33.

Negatively: God Is Not Pleased with Confusion

The beginning of this verse gives us our first clue to God's character.

> For God is not a God of confusion but of peace.
> (v. 33a)

The word *confusion* means "disorder" or "unrest." It may also be described as a "disruption of the peace of the community . . . by orgiastic impulses [unrestrained emotions] in the gatherings of the congregation."[1] God does not find pleasure in worship services where individual impulsiveness obscures His holy character.

Positively: God Is Pleased with Order

The last part of verse 33 tells us what God does prefer.

> [God is a God] of peace, as in all the churches of the saints.

The context surrounding this verse shows us that God is pleased when things are done in a well-organized manner. He's pleased with an assembly that is well-managed; with a body of believers who exhibit self-control and use their gifts, talents, and skills for the purpose of strengthening the church (see vv. 3, 12, 26, 31). As Paul reiterates in verse 40,

> All things must be done properly and in an orderly manner.

Do you doubt that? Then spend a few hours with a microscope or a telescope to observe the Creator's incredible organization of the universe![2]

---

1. Gerhard Kittel, ed., *Theological Dictionary of the New Testament,* trans. and ed. Geoffrey W. Bromiley (Grand Rapids, Mich.: William B. Eerdmans Publishing Co., 1965), vol. 3, p. 446.

2. This is not to imply that a display of emotion signifies a lack of control and is therefore wrong. Not at all. We just need to remember our goal of building up one another in Christ. Church is a place and time for heartfelt worship, confession, prayer, instruction, encouragement—it should never be mistaken for a mundane corporate board meeting of bored stockholders.

Principles for Good Leadership

The life of Moses also speak to church leaders. In fact, an entire chapter in Exodus is devoted to the subject of his leadership style. In this chapter, we will see Moses' need for organization and how God used a wise man to teach him, and us, some important principles for good leadership.

An Evaluation

When Jethro, Moses' father-in-law, visits the Israelites' camp and hears all that God has done on their behalf, he responds with joyful praise.

> So Jethro said, "Blessed be the Lord who delivered you from the hand of the Egyptians and from the hand of Pharaoh, and who delivered the people from under the hand of the Egyptians. Now I know that the Lord is greater than all the gods; indeed, it was proven when they dealt proudly against the people." (Exod. 18:10–11)

The next day, however, when Moses gets back to work, Jethro sits back and observes his son-in-law.

> It came about the next day that Moses sat to judge the people, and the people stood about Moses from the morning until the evening. (v. 13)

Jethro frowns with displeasure when he sees Moses attempting to meet the needs of too many people by himself. And he lets Moses know how he feels.

> Now when Moses' father-in-law saw all that he was doing for the people, he said, "What is this thing that you are doing for the people? Why do you alone sit as judge and all the people stand about you from morning until evening?" (v. 14)

Does this question remind you of any leader you might know? Is that leader or his congregation tempted to keep adding things to the schedule that threaten to pull that person under? If so, the following counsel from Jethro may help keep all of your heads above water.

Some Truths to Remember

> Moses' father-in-law said to him, "The thing that
> you are doing is not good. You will surely wear out,
> both yourself and these people who are with you,
> for the task is too heavy for you; you cannot do it
> alone." (vv. 17–18)

Jethro is basically saying that *one person, no matter how gifted, cannot do a big job all alone.* A gifted person can do a lot, but no person is gifted enough to run a ministry alone. It may appear very spiritual to be overworked, but remember: God is pleased when things are done in a well-ordered way—in a way that brings exhilaration, not exhaustion.

Jethro knows the problem is serious enough that he needs to say something to Moses.

> "Now listen to me: I will give you counsel, and God
> be with you. You be the people's representative be-
> fore God, and you bring the disputes to God, then
> teach them the statutes and the laws, and make
> known to them the way in which they are to walk
> and the work they are to do." (vv. 19–20)

In essence, Jethro counsels that *high-visibility leadership is still needed, but that role must be limited.* His advice sounds like it came straight from one of today's management seminars. But rather than being a trendy business fad, this lasting word of God is true in all ages and in all leadership roles, including pastoring a church. Freeing up our leaders from smaller, time-consuming tasks allows them to focus on the big picture, seek and make plans to implement God's plan for the ministry, and truly lead.

Jethro has two things in mind as he gives Moses his advice—the work has to get done, and the leader needs relief.

> "Furthermore, you shall select out of all the people
> able men who fear God, men of truth, those who
> hate dishonest gain; and you shall place these over
> them as leaders of thousands, of hundreds, of fifties
> and of tens. Let them judge the people at all times;
> and let it be that every major dispute they will bring
> to you, but every minor dispute they themselves will
> judge. So it will be easier for you, and they will bear
> the burden with you." (vv. 21–22)

The truth from this counsel is: *Big loads must be borne by many, and the helpers must be selected carefully.* Where did we get the idea that Maalox, Alka-Seltzer, and Excedrin are the executive symbols of spiritual success? Why should we believe that working in God's vineyard is backbreaking labor, without a moment's leisure? If doing God's work becomes a burden, then the load needs to be properly distributed.

But not to just anybody. Jethro specifies that these people must be "able," or skilled, for the task. They must also fear God and have integrity—be people who will refuse to compromise when decisions need to be made. And finally, they must "hate dishonest gain." Their focus cannot be on money.

What a difference well-chosen workers might have made in the church of Ephesus—helping the leader keep the love of Christ first and foremost in the people's hearts. Or in the churches of Pergamum and Thyatira—where the pastor and his helpers together could have steered the people clear of false teachers.

The result of work delegated to qualified helpers is a peaceful, stable, organized ministry that pleases and can be used effectively by God.

> "If you do this thing and God so commands you,
> then you will be able to endure, and all these people
> also will go to their place in peace." (v. 23)

Proper pastoral management brings about two things: leaders don't wear out, and harmony prevails. And like the church at Philadelphia, a healthy church will be able to make the most of the opportunities God brings their way.

Needed Changes

To Moses' credit, he didn't try to justify his leadership style or get defensive about it. Instead, he listened to his father-in-law's wise counsel and followed through on it.

> So Moses listened to his father-in-law and did
> all that he had said. Moses chose able men out of
> all Israel and made them heads over the people,
> leaders of thousands, of hundreds, of fifties and of
> tens. (vv. 24–25)

Moses matched the jobs to the people's abilities—some were able to lead thousands, others just a handful. But each took a share of the load, and the result was a success.

> They judged the people at all times; the difficult
> dispute they would bring to Moses, but every minor
> dispute they themselves would judge. (v. 26)

These people were not chosen just because they were willing to do the work or because they were the most popular. They were chosen because their attitudes and abilities matched the tasks to be done. Moses' load was lightened, burnout was left begging at the door, and harmony prevailed in Israel's camp.

Reminders to Those Who Select Leaders

Here are three principles to help you evaluate how you can properly select leaders in your church.

The selection of officers and pastoral staff is a serious business. The positions of leadership within a church are not to be given or taken lightly. They are not rewards for the beautiful, the popular, or the rich. Study the qualifications Paul lists in Titus 1:5–9.

> For this reason I left you in Crete, that you would
> set in order what remains and appoint elders in every
> city as I directed you, namely, if any man is above
> reproach, the husband of one wife, having children
> who believe, not accused of dissipation or rebellion.
> For the overseer must be above reproach as God's
> steward, not self-willed, not quick-tempered, not ad-
> dicted to wine, not pugnacious, not fond of sordid
> gain, but hospitable, loving what is good, sensible,
> just, devout, self-controlled, holding fast the faithful
> word which is in accordance with the teaching, so
> that he will be able both to exhort in sound doctrine
> and to refute those who contradict.

If the church is to be effectively led, effective leaders must be chosen according to the guidelines established in Scripture. Character, not social status, reflects godly leadership.

Those who become leaders automatically become models. Hebrews 13:7 encourages us to emulate our leaders' lives.

> Remember those who led you, who spoke the
> word of God to you; and considering the result of
> their conduct, imitate their faith.

It is not enough to choose officers, pastors, and leaders simply because they are efficient organizers. Models are needed! Models who can instruct us. Models who can inspire us. Models we can imitate in the whole of our lives.

Those we select, we must willingly follow. Our leaders will impact us and our families for years to come. They will offer counsel according to the kind of people they are. Selecting qualified leaders will secure godly direction even for difficult days ahead—but we must be willing to get behind the leaders we choose in order for godly vision to become reality.

> Obey your leaders and submit to them, for they
> keep watch over your souls as those who will give an
> account. Let them do this with joy and not with grief,
> for this would be unprofitable for you. (Heb. 13:17)

Significant ministries are sustained by faithful, consistent, dedicated leadership, the kind modeled by men and women in Scripture who served with integrity, refusing to lag behind because of pressure, demands, or ingratitude.

As you step into leadership or help select those who will serve, take time to examine and apply God's principles regarding character. And remember Jethro's advice—seek ways to lighten your leaders' overloaded schedules. That way, they'll become more effective, the body will become better equipped, and the church will honor the One by whose name she is called and who watches over her for His saving name's sake.

 Living Insights

In John 12:21, some Greeks coming to Jerusalem to observe the Passover asked one of Jesus' disciples, "Sir, we wish to see Jesus."

In essence, the whole world pleads this same question in its frenzied search for love and meaning. But where is Jesus today? How can anyone see Him? The Scriptures teach that *we* are to be His representatives—that everyone who knows the Lord Jesus as Savior is being transformed into His likeness. And nowhere should He be more evident than in the lives of the leaders of His church. As Gene Getz has said, "A person who has become a man of God through a process of spiritual growth and development over a period of time . . . has learned to reflect Jesus Christ in his total life-style."[3]

Let's take a moment to examine the specific character traits of a Christlike leader. Read Titus 1:5–9 and 1 Timothy 3:1–7, and list the traits that you find there.

Category   **Christlike Traits**

Character   _____

_____

Family   _____

_____

Maturity   _____

_____

Reputation   _____

_____

Are you a leader? In the home? At work? In the church? A parachurch ministry? A secular organization? What are your leadership strengths as defined in the previous passages?

_____

_____

_____

_____

_____

_____

3. Gene A. Getz, *The Measure of a Man* (Glendale, Calif.: Gospel Light Publications, Regal Books, 1974), p. 16.

What needs work? How? Name at least three practical ways you can improve for the sake of the One whose image you project.

_____

_____

_____

_____

_____

_____

_____

_____

_____

BOOKS FOR PROBING FURTHER

I t has been a privilege to have pastors and teachers such as John Stott, Leon Morris, Robert Mounce, and William Barclay as companions throughout this study. Like the wise men of Proverbs 13:20, they have mentored us along the way in the timeless wisdom of Christ's letters to the seven churches. Perhaps you would like to travel further with these men and others like them in your own study of Revelation. Let me introduce you to . . .

Barclay, William. *The Revelation of John*. Revised edition. The Daily Study Bible Series. Philadelphia, Pa.: Westminster Press, 1976. Vol. 1. Commentary.

Johnson, Alan F. "Revelation." In *The Expositor's Bible Commentary*. Gen. ed. Frank E. Gaebelein. Grand Rapids, Mich.: Zondervan Publishing House, Regency Reference Library, 1981. Vol. 12. Commentary.

Morris, Leon. *The Book of Revelation: An Introduction and Commentary*. The Tyndale New Testament Commentaries series. 1987. Reprint, Grand Rapids, Mich.: William B. Eerdmans Publishing Co., 1996. Commentary.

Mounce, Robert H. *The Book of Revelation*. The New International Commentary on the New Testament Series. Grand Rapids, Mich.: William B. Eerdmans Publishing Co., 1977. Commentary.

Peterson, Eugene H. *Reversed Thunder: The Revelation of John and the Praying Imagination*. San Francisco, Calif.: HarperSanFrancisco, 1988. Meditative commentary.

Ramsay, W. M. Ed. Mark W. Wilson. *The Letters to the Seven Churches*. Updated edition. Peabody, Mass.: Hendrickson Publishers, 1994. Commentary on Revelation 1–3.

Ramsey, James B. *The Book of Revelation*. 1873. Reprint, Carlisle, Pa.: Banner of Truth Trust, 1995. Exposition of Revelation 1–11.

Stott, John. *What Christ Thinks of the Church*. Wheaton, Ill.: Harold Shaw Publishers, 1990. Commentary on Revelation 1–3.

Walvoord, John F. "Revelation." In *The Bible Knowledge Commentary*. New Testament edition. Ed. John F. Walvoord and Roy B. Zuck. Wheaton, Ill.: Scripture Press Publications, Victor Books, 1983. Commentary.

Wilcock, Michael. *The Message of Revelation: I Saw Heaven Opened*. The Bible Speaks Today Series. Downers Grove, Ill.: InterVarsity Press, 1975. Commentary.

Some of the books listed may be out of print and available only through a library. For those currently available, please contact your local Christian bookstore. Books by Charles R. Swindoll may be obtained through Insight for Living, as well as some books by other authors. Just call the IFL office that serves you.

NOTES

NOTES

NOTES